Compassion and Education

Andrew Peterson

Compassion and Education

Cultivating Compassionate Children, Schools and Communities

Andrew Peterson
Faculty of Education
Canterbury Christ Church University
Canterbury, United Kingdom

ISBN 978-1-137-54837-5   ISBN 978-1-137-54838-2 (eBook)
DOI 10.1057/978-1-137-54838-2

Library of Congress Control Number: 2016951863

Cover illustration: Cover image © Mint Images RF/ Getty Images

Printed on acid-free paper

This Palgrave Macmillan imprint is published by Springer Nature
The registered company is Macmillan Publishers Ltd.
The registered company address is: The Campus, 4 Crinan Street, London, N1 9XW, United Kingdom

For Jessica, Oliver and George

ACKNOWLEDGEMENTS

I have many people to thank for their help and support with this book. The idea for a book examining compassion as a virtue developed from my previous work on global citizenship, and from reflecting on those virtues someone we might characterise as a "global citizen" could possess. An invitation to provide a keynote at an annual international CitizED conference at the University of Birmingham in 2014 provided an opportunity to start thinking in detail about compassion and education, so first my thanks go to the organisers of that conference and the colleagues in attendance who provided their thoughts on compassion.

Second, I would like to thank colleagues at the University of South Australia who acted as sounding boards for my initial ideas, and helped to shape these in certain directions. In particular, I am indebted to Greg Bowyer, Julie Trinidad, Brendan Bentley and Rob Hattam. Third, I owe a great deal of thanks to my colleagues and friends – Laura D'Olimpio, Trevor Cooling and Bob Bowie – who have provided valuable feedback on draft chapters. Their thoughts were warmly provided and gratefully received, though of course any errors are mine and mine alone. Finally, I would like to thank my family – Jessica, Oliver and George – for their love, support and welcome thoughts about various ideas in the book discussed over the dinner table.

I was fortunate to receive an ARC DECRA (DE150100926) research fellowship which enabled me to devote time to the ideas contained within the book during 2015 when these were in their formative stages and wish to also acknowledge my thanks for this here.

CONTENTS

CHAPTER 1

Introduction

For whatever reasons suffering appears to be a condition of human[1] existence, it is at least a condition visible to us in many forms. What is more, human suffering may well be on the increase. In 1991, James Grant (cited in Moeller 1999, p. 8), then executive director of UNICEF, made the following assertion in the context of recent natural disasters, diseases and wars: 'these really are the most severe set of problems one can remember coming at one time since the end of World War II.' Fast forward 25 years to the present day. We too live in times dominated by suffering caused by natural disasters, conflicts and disease. Indeed, reminiscent of Grant's sentiments, the United Nations Humanitarian Summit (UNPF 2016) was held in May 2016 in a context in which:

> The world is at a critical juncture. We are witnessing the highest level of human suffering since the Second World War. Nearly 60 million people, half of them children, have been forced from their homes due to conflict and violence. The human and economic cost of disasters caused by natural hazards is also escalating. In the last two decades, 218 million people each year were affected by disasters; at an annual cost to the global economy that now exceeds $300 billion.

Given that the suffering of others is a visible feature of our daily lives, what sort of response to suffering might be of value? One way of approaching an answer to this question would be to focus on collective, often large-scale responses as typically expressed through humanitarian aid. Another way

© The Author(s) 2017
A. Peterson, *Compassion and Education*,
DOI 10.1057/978-1-137-54838-2_1

1

would be to concentrate on immediate personal and individual responses to suffering, mediated by the various communities in which that individual stands and through which both individual and collective responses may be formed. Central to both of these responses is a particular moral concept – compassion.

Yet, compassion is not straightforward and unambiguous term and certainly it is a concept which some have felt a need to reject. What we mean by compassion therefore requires elucidating and justifying. Further, how we enact compassion (and therefore any educational attempts to cultivate compassion) will depend on the precise way in which it is conceived. With this in mind, I offer from the outset the following definition of compassion which I seek to explore and defend in this book:

Compassion is a virtue, one which can be understood as a cognitive, emotional and volitional response to the suffering of others. Compassion is based on a recognition and appreciation of common humanity, including humanity's fragility. It requires empathic distress, care for others, and can inform and lead to actions in support of others. Compassion represents an expression of ourselves and our humanity, and relates to notions of the good life and human flourishing.

To be compassionate requires us to *recognise* and *care about* the suffering of others and, on this basis, to take some form of appropriate action in response. While often immediate and proximal, the scope of compassion is universal, taking in the whole of humanity. A precise feature of compassion is that its object is someone, or some group, with whom we may or may not stand in some immediate relationship but to whom we come into relation by virtue of compassion. While compassion may involve relationships between teacher and pupil, health-care worker and patient, politician and constituent, it may also operate between strangers.

Compassion has been, and remains, a significant concept for explorations of the human condition. In recent years compassion has featured widely within public discourse – often represented and re-presented through various media. Yet, compassion is used, supported and rejected for various reasons and in a multitude of ways. Compassion is, therefore, a concept which at once appears important, but also somewhat ambiguous. For some, compassion is also troubling, as it can become permeated by unequal, patronising standpoints. Indeed, citing the recent 'rehabilitation' of compassion as a key political virtue, Ure and Frost (2014, p. 2) point to the fact that 'compassion has been hailed as both the key democratic virtue and condemned as politically toxic'.

Given the current prominence of compassion and these conceptual issues, for those like myself who wish to suggest that compassion is an essential and positive concept for the public and private lives of citizens today, it is necessary to engage with certain central questions, including the following:

1. What sort of concept is compassion, and what are its key features?
2. How does compassion relate to other affective concepts, such as pity, sympathy, empathy, care and love?
3. What does compassion ask of us in relation to others and how do we enact this?
4. How does compassion relate to notions of the self?

This book is interested in these questions about compassion, but it is so in regard to cultivating compassion through education. For this reason, it will also engage with related questions about the ways in which compassion and education do, and can, intersect.

Calls to Compassion

At the time this book was being written, calls to compassion have become common in a range of contexts. Some such calls are detailed below, but can initially be illustrated in debates about appropriate responses to the Europe Migrant Crisis and the Global Refugee Crisis. Many commentators, including religious leaders, have prefaced their support or rejection of particular responses on the basis of 'compassion'. In the UK, for example, Right Reverend David Walker (2015), the Anglican Bishop of Manchester, called on politicians to 'look on migrants with compassion', as 'human beings' rather than 'criminals'. This appeal was echoed by the Senior Rabbi, Julia Neuberger (2015), who in arguing that viewing migrants as criminals was 'shameful', suggested not just that migrants should receive compassion, but that they *deserve* compassion.

While we may agree with these sentiments, it is another matter what compassionate policy responses might actually be. For both Walker and Neuberger, a compassionate response is one (1) in which migrants are admitted and welcomed to the UK and other European nations; (2) which seeks to understand why they have fled their homes, and risked their lives in doing so; and furthermore, (3) which involves political leaders (in this case those within Europe and their allies) in accepting their own share of responsibility for the crises. Yet, in other contexts alternative responses to migration have been enacted on the premise of 'compassion'. Most notably, the then Australian Prime Minister, Tony Abbott, proclaimed the success of the Federal Government's Operation Sovereign Borders (known commonly as Stop the Boats), the policy enacted since 2013 which aims to stop migrants entering Australia by sea. In spite of criticism that the policy is in breach of the United Nations Refugee Convention[2] (see, e.g., Doherty 2014; Joseph 2015), Abbott (AAP 2014) referred to Operation Sovereign Borders as 'the most decent and compassionate thing th[e] government had done'. Following the drowning of over a thousand migrants in the Mediterranean Sea, Abbott (Dearden 2015) advised European leaders that 'the only way you can stop the deaths is, in fact, to stop the boats'. Clearly, compassion can mean different things to different people and can be put to work in support of different actions.

While perhaps the most high profile, these brief vignettes are not the only available ones which illustrate recent calls to compassion. Other calls to compassion in public life are not hard to find, and they include the following:

1. In recent years politicians in the UK have called for the adoption of social values and policies based on compassion alongside neo-liberal economic approaches. These calls were particularly evident in the days following the General Election in May 2015, then Conservative Prime Minister David Cameron told the first cabinet of the newly elected government that any change to public services should be based on 'true social justice and genuine compassion' (BBC 2015a). Reflecting on the defeat of the Labour party in the election, former leader and Prime Minister Tony Blair advocated that the party needed to become a 'party of ambition as well as compassion' (Blair 2015), while the then deputy chairperson of the UK Independence Party argued that the party needed to focus more on 'compassionate, centre-ground' policies

(*The Guardian* 2015a). In 2015, Labour MP Liam Byrne (2015) called on the UK government to include compassion within its list of fundamental British values, tabling the following Early Day Motion for debate in the House of Commons:

> That this house notes the list of British values published in the Prevent Strategy 2011 includes democracy, the rule of law, individual liberty and mutual respect and tolerance of different faiths and beliefs; believes that 'compassion' is a fundamental British value which our government should affirm and our schools seek to actively promote; and calls for the Government to add 'compassion' to the official definition of British values[3];

2. The concept of 'compassionate conservatism' has developed as a particular response to how centrist-leaning political conservatives should approach social values and policies. Books in the UK – such as Jesse Norman and Janan Ganesh's (2006) *Compassionate conservatism: What it is, why we need it* – and in the USA – such as Marvin Olasky's (2000) *Compassionate conservatism: What it is, what it does and how can it transform America* – have offered compassionate conservatism as a response to social issues;

3. Following a series of events and reports in the late 2000s and early 2010s which questioned the quality of healthcare within the UK National Health Service, it was widely proclaimed that nurses, midwives and other healthcare workers needed to be more compassionate in the care of patients (see, e.g., HSO 2011; Francis 2013). In late 2012 the Department of Health (2012) published a vision and strategy entitled 'Compassion in Practice'. The document defines compassion as 'how care is given through relationships based on empathy, respect and dignity – it can also be described as intelligent kindness, and is central to how people perceive their care' (DoH 2012, p. 13). Within it, the Chief Nursing Officer for England made clear the need to 'change the way we work, transform the care of our patients and ensure we deliver a culture of compassionate care' (DoH 2012, p. 6). The term 'compassionate care' is now central to the work of the NHS;

4. In 2008, Karen Armstrong was awarded the TED prize and used this to produce the *Charter for Compassion*, which in turn formed the basis of the global Charter for Compassion organisation and movement aimed at encouraging people around the world to embrace the principle of compassion. The Charter[4] commences as follows:

The principle of compassion lies at the heart of all religious, ethical and spiritual traditions, calling us always to treat all others as we wish to be treated ourselves. Compassion impels us to work tirelessly to alleviate the suffering of our fellow creatures, to dethrone ourselves from the centre of our world and put another there, and to honour the inviolable sanctity of every single human being, treating everybody, without exception, with absolute justice, equity and respect.

It calls upon:

all men and women to restore compassion to the centre of morality and religion ~ to return to the ancient principle that any interpretation of scripture that breeds violence, hatred or disdain is illegitimate ~ to ensure that youth are given accurate and respectful information about other traditions, religions and cultures ~ to encourage a positive appreciation of cultural and religious diversity ~ to cultivate an informed empathy with the suffering of all human beings – even those regarded as enemies.

A central tenet of *Charter for Compassion* is that embracing and enacting compassion is essential for a just and peaceful world. In addition, the *Charter for Compassion* presents compassion as a practically acquired knowledge, something which can be developed and learnt through practice and reflection.

These calls to compassion are an important feature of public life, and in various ways inform the focus and interests with which this book is concerned. But, while the calls to compassion highlighted here are high-profile and significant, they do not represent the totality of the ways compassion features in everyday lives. To some extent – though not entirely – calls to compassion involve a degree of forethought and planning which can detract from the spontaneity often involved in compassionate relationships between fellow humans. While much harder to quantify, compassion is likely to be an important feature of the ways in which people qua human beings engage with others – directly and indirectly, explicitly and implicitly – and as such is a quality of our everyday lived experiences that one cannot, and should not, always expect and plan for.

At times, unforeseen everyday compassionate acts that begin on a fundamentally human level enter the public sphere. In 2015, Alan Barnes, a 67-year old man with disabilities living in the North East of England was subjected to physical assault with intent to robbery close to his home. Hearing of the incident, a local beautician, Katie Cutler, launched a twitter appeal in the hope of raising £500 to support Alan Barnes. The appeal raised £330,000 and Katie Cutler has gone on to establish a charitable foundation. In reporting the trial of the perpetrator, a local paper, *The Northern Echo*, wrote that 'what we will all remember most about this story is the compassion which was inspired by an act of violence' (Barren 2015).

This example evidences that compassion is often sparked by a particular incident of suffering, one which ignites our compassion for others. This is not to say that calls to compassion are altogether misguided – far from it. But rather is to suggest that often compassion, and compassionate acts, require some sense of inspiration which is likely to result not from persuasion, argument or rhetoric, but from a particular stimulus which engages the heart and mind in a way that compels one to action on the basis of a sense of shared, common humanity and a genuine concern for others. The impact of the image of Alan Kurdi lying face down on a Turkish beach further illustrates the importance of shared humanity and concern (the picture was shared on Twitter with the hashtag #kiyiyavuraninsanlik /#humanitywashedashore). The picture changed perceptions of both politicians and public – and not just because of the suffering involved, but also because of its expression of the fragility of human life. The day after the image was published, then UK Prime Minister David Cameron suggested that 'anyone who saw those pictures overnight could not help but be moved' and that 'Britain is a moral nation and we will fulfil our moral responsibilities' (Dathan 2015). Subsequently Cameron announced to Parliament that the UK would resettle 20,000 refugees from Syrian camps over the following 5 years. Again in the UK, the hashtag #refugeeswelcome surged following the image's publication in the mainstream media (Devichand 2016). Similar trends were witnessed in other European nations. According to Peter Bouckaert, emergencies director for Human Rights Watch, the power of the image lies to a large part in the fact that 'for a lot of the public, their first reaction is: "This could have been my child" ' (Laurent 2015).

While compassion can be viewed as a capacity of which all humans are capable, it is not difficult to accept that people can and often do resort to different (im)moral responses to the suffering of others than compassion – indeed, there may be times in which we all chose a path different to compassion in specific contexts. Few of us are likely to be fully moral saints or moral sinners. This means that someone, for example, who is a scoundrel in some areas of their life may, legitimately, be compassionate in others. This idea was famously proposed by Adam Smith ([1759] 2009, p. 13), who commenced *The Theory of Moral Sentiments* with the following:

> How selfish soever man may be supposed, there are evidently some principles in his nature, which interest him in the fortune of others, and render their happiness necessary to him, though he derives nothing from it except the pleasure of seeing it. Of this kind is pity or compassion, the emotion which we feel for the misery of others, when we either see it, or are made to conceive it in a very lively manner. That we often derive sorrow from the sorrow of others, is a matter of fact too obvious to require any instances to prove it; for this sentiment, like all other original passions of human nature, is by no means confined to the virtuous and humane, though they perhaps may feel it with the most exquisite sensibility. The greatest ruffian, the most hardened violator of the laws of society, is not altogether without it.

Compassion, then, is just *one* response to suffering that may be enacted – there are many others. This means that as well as exploring *why* people may be compassionate and *why* people may choose to be compassionate over other available options, we also need to consider ways in which compassion can be *inhibited*, including those factors (individual or contextually specific) which can serve to limit compassion for others. Allied to this is the suggestion that in and of itself compassion is not an easy attribute (or virtue as I will later argue) to possess and to express, and that as such compassion is learned, reflected upon and expressed in contextually sensitive ways. As the Catholic theologian Henri Nouwen (2009, p. 18) reminds us,

> Let us not underestimate how hard it is to be compassionate. Compassion is hard because it requires the inner disposition to go with others to places where they are weak, vulnerable, lonely, and broken. But this is not our spontaneous response to suffering. What we desire most is to do away with suffering by fleeing from it or finding a quick cure for it

One need not accept the full force of Nouwen's position to agree with the idea that compassion is difficult, and often places us in situations which challenge us.

Moreover, and given the complexities at hand, educating for compassion is likely to be a somewhat messy affair, one which is unlikely to occur in linear trajectories. With this recognition in mind, part of my concern in writing this book is to suggest there is a danger that the increasing use of compassion in public discourse – starting to be mirrored in educational circles – may render compassion as something general, ill-defined and somewhat ubiquitous. That is, we are in danger of compassion becoming over-used to refer to any feeling or act which could be conceived of as good, caring or kind, or used by commentators to justify or impel certain actions without critical appreciation of what compassion *actually* requires of us. Reflecting on the use of compassion in American political and public discourse (compassion became a term used by both Democrats and Republicans), Garber (2004, p. 17) warns that '"compassion" these days is a "liberal" word, damned with faint praise from both the right and the left'. Under such conditions, compassion may lack real meaning.

Similarly, there is an associated tension. This is that when compassion is used to refer to something more akin with kindness, empathy or some such other prosocial behaviour the actual meanings of these terms (and indeed their relation to compassion) can become compromised. While concepts such as kindness, empathy, care and sympathy may be constituent parts of compassion – indeed they are each important steps on the pathway towards compassion – none are direct synonyms. That is, while such terms are necessary for compassion none alone are sufficient for it. In making this point one has to tread a careful line. I am certainly not suggesting that kindness, empathy, care and sympathy and other associated concepts with which this book is concerned are not important in their own right. Far from it. I am suggesting, however, that compassion requires something more than any of these terms, alone, can provide.

In advancing these initial remarks it is important to state that there are not necessarily hard and fast rules about what responses are or are not compassionate. Indeed, it may be more straightforward to identify acts which lack compassion than it is to fully specify those which are compassionate. In this sense, compassion is not only a contested term, but is one with fuzzy edges. This means that rather than searching for concrete answers about what compassion is and what a compassionate response may be in any given context, a more appropriate stance – one which this book seeks to adopt – is to enter into deliberation about compassion in a way which engages with the concept's blurry nature.

COMPASSION AND EDUCATION

Alongside this interest in compassion in wider public life, education has increasingly been identified as a crucial mechanism in cultivating compassion (see, e.g., Arnot et al. 2009; Wilde 2013; Coles 2015a; Taggart 2016). My focus in this present book lies in particular on the cultivation of compassion within the education of young children in schools. Compassion is a phrase which can be found within a number of important fields of education, including character education, positive psychology, wellbeing, mindfulness, global citizenship, religious education and values education. In addition, schools engage with and educate compassion in a variety of ways – for example, through school ethos and values, teacher–student and student–student relationships, extra-curricular activities, as well as through curricular content.

It should also be stated from the outset that it would, of course, be wrong to claim that schools are the *primary* factor in cultivating compassion. Other social units – including parents, families, peer-groups, the media, religious groups and community organisations – play an important part in cultivating (or indeed not cultivating) compassionate children. However, schools clearly *do* play a role in developing the moral, social and political capabilities of young people – including how they understand and express compassion. Moreover, schools do (or at least as this book argues, should) engage in various ways with other social units – including the family – in order to cultivate compassion. Yet, while there are claims that education needs to take compassion seriously, and there are increasing amounts of educational initiatives which seek to support the teaching of compassion in schools,[5] there remains a limited amount of educational research which explores in depth what compassion actually is, what its central tenets are and how these relate to the cultivation of compassion in schools. Again, and similarly within public discourse, there is a danger that compassion within education may become simultaneously ubiquitous yet under-defined; of the utmost importance yet hard to pin down in practice.

In recognising this danger, this book aims to provide a detailed analysis of what compassion – understood here as a virtue – comprises and entails. It seeks to offer an account of compassion which is educationally relevant, not only in the ideas it sets out, but also in the spirit of provoking further critique, deliberation and analysis from others. At the heart of the book are the following two contentions: First, that compassion can play a central role in our lives as humans and citizens, relating as it does to notions of common humanity, care for others and what it means to live a good life. Second, and for this reason, that compassion represents a possible and important focus for educational endeavours, one which should be cultivated through both direct teaching and wider schools values and processes. These contentions inter-relate in essential ways given that how we conceive compassion will necessarily shape its expression within educational discourse and practice.

Following this introduction, the book comprises seven chapters. In Chap. 2, the core elements of compassion are explored, and it is argued that compassion is best understood as a virtue comprising particular emotional, cognitive and active responses which recognise common humanity with one's fellow humans. In Chap. 3, the emotional aspects of compassion are examined, and in particular pity, sympathy and empathy. While recognising the limitations of certain versions of each of emotional response to suffering, it will be suggested that each stand in important relation with compassion. The focus of Chap. 4 is compassionate responses. In this chapter various actions engendered by recognising the suffering of others are explored. The chapter also considers barriers to compassion. In Chap. 5, the potentially thorny issue of self in compassion is considered. In some ways, the view that compassion involves regard for oneself could be seen to be an Achilles heel for compassion given that the concept is typically valued for the extent to which it is other-regarding. Taking the challenge of self-interest seriously, it is argued that compassion justifiably includes some form of regard for one self. Chapters 6 and 7 both build on the arguments forwarded in the preceding chapters to explore their implications for educational curricular and practice. Chapter 6 focuses specifically on teaching about and for compassion, while Chap. 7 examines compassion in relation to wider school cultures and practices, including through partnerships with families and communities.

I would like to conclude this introduction with two further points – one core to the argument I seek to make throughout the book and one about the spirit in which this book is offered. I wish to argue that compassion is important because it relates both to others and ourselves. Compassion says something about the way in which we value others, ourselves and our relationships with others. In important ways, compassion relates to ideas of the good life and human flourishing – what human flourishing means to and for us, and what it means to and for others. When we conceive compassion as a virtue, the connection to the good life becomes clearer, and education becomes an important process through which young people can come to understand, explore, recognise and value compassion as forming part of a virtuous life. Second, a key argument of this book is that dialogue provides a crucial way through which we relate with others about compassion, suffering and notions of the good life. I believe that dialogue – understood broadly – can play a key role in bringing us closer to others in ways which benefit not only our understanding or others but also our care for others. With this in mind, the arguments offered in this book are done so in the spirit of dialogue, and with the hope that others who read them will respond with their own thoughts and contentions, drawing on their own conceptions of what it means to be a good person and to live a good life.

NOTES

1. My focus in this book is specifically on compassion as a human property in relation to other humans. I, therefore, am not seeking to make any claims about whether compassion is possible, or otherwise, towards other animals or for other categories, such as the environment.
2. In February 2016, the Australian High Court upheld the constitutionality of detaining asylum seekers offshore (Hurst and Doherty 2016).
3. http://liambyrne.co.uk/edm-on-compassion-as-a-fundamental-british-value/
4. http://www.charterforcompassion.org/index.php/charter/charter-overvew
5. see, for example, http://www.mindwithheart.org.uk/; https://www.facing history.org/; http://www.seedsofcompassion.org/; http://www.caritas.org.au/learn/schools.

CHAPTER 2

The Virtue of Compassion

INTRODUCTION

In the history of political thought compassion is a concept that has garnered positive attention from some while being critiqued and dismissed by others. This has meant that while there has been an enduring interest in compassion, the concept remains inherently contested. The condition in which compassion finds itself can readily be identified. A number of Western philosophers have placed compassion as central to morality. Compassion forms a cornerstone of theological morality, most notably within Christianity and Buddhism. However, compassion has certainly had its critics, as exemplified in Nietzsche's treatment of compassion (*Mitleid*) as essentially self-serving. White (2008, p. 39) summarises the treatment of compassion in Western philosophy in the following terms:

> for the most part Western philosophers tend to look down on compassion since it is held to be more of a feeling than a determination of the will (and hence we appear to have less control over it); and because it seems to increase the amount of misery in the world by making us share in the sufferings of others.

The aim of this second chapter, therefore, is to explore the basic features of compassion and, in doing so, to argue that compassion is best understood as a moral virtue. Compassion is, though, a particular kind of moral virtue. It is a moral virtue which while stemming from an emotional response

© The Author(s) 2017
A. Peterson, *Compassion and Education*,
DOI 10.1057/978-1-137-54838-2_2

admits both cognitive and volitional dimensions. To develop these suggestions, the chapter is structured around three main sections. In the first some basic and fundamental premises are offered for conceiving compassion as involving, but as being more than, a strictly emotional response. Identifying the crucial relationship within compassion between emotions, reasons and action, the second section focuses on practical wisdom as a way of understanding the integral inter-relationship which lies at the heart of compassion. The third section builds on the two previous sections to examine the nature of human relations central to compassion, and it is argued again that these are crucial to conceiving compassion as a virtue on the basis that they involve a commitment to human flourishing.

COMPASSION – MORE THAN A FEELING

In exploring the concept of gratitude, David Carr (2015, p. 1477) reminds us that 'while (even) positive emotions, sentiments and feelings are necessary parts or constituents of virtue, more is needed for them to qualify as virtues'. This is true of compassion. A key concern of this chapter, therefore, is to examine what it is about compassion that takes it beyond a simply emotional response. This is not, of course, to deny the centrality of emotions to compassion. Compassion is a virtue which not only includes the affective, but stems directly from it. We frequently say, for example, that we *feel* compassion for others. To remove emotions from compassion would not only be to negate its applicability as a virtue – it would be to render compassion meaningless. Indeed, so integral are emotions to compassion that there has been some tendency to view compassion solely in emotional terms (cf. Faulkner 2014b). Even in work that seeks to extend compassion beyond simply an emotional state and response, emotion remains front and centre in a definitional sense. Berlant (2004, p. 5; original emphasis), for example, refers to compassion as '*an emotion in operation*', while Crisp (2008) considers compassion as *both* an emotion and a virtue.

Emotions, then, are central to compassion. But compassion clearly involves other faculties – faculties which I suggest are important in conceiving the concept in terms of a virtue. Now, it may be claimed that I am putting the cart before the horse in seeking to understand the ways in which compassion involves *more than a feeling* without specifying precisely what the central features of that feeling are (which is the focus of the next chapter). However, in this instance, and to follow the proverb through, I think there is good reason to start with the cart before investigating the horse. Not least, understanding the various facets – the affective, cognitive and volitional – which comprise compassion seems a necessary and important starting point before each can undergo more detailed exploration.

It may be asked from the outset, of course, *why* certain feelings (say, empathy[1] or sympathy) require something further in order to constitute essentially moral concepts or, indeed, virtues (say, compassion). For, if it is the case that a given emotion relating to fellow-feeling can do the moral work I am seeking to attribute to compassion, then the project I am attempting here would be fatally flawed. Why, then, do we need a concept of compassion rather than, say, sympathy or empathy? The answer to this question lies initially in the extent to which the particular emotions concerned – in our case sympathy or empathy – can be said to be useful moral concepts. Here, so far as both sympathy and empathy are concerned, there appear to be important reasons for questioning whether either is, in and of itself, a moral concept, particularly one of the morally good kind.

Let us say, for instance, that Molly feels empathy for Sally. On a simple understanding of empathy we can understand this as involving Molly with appreciating what Sally feels (or at least seeking to), something which Sally and Molly may or may not find uncomfortable (I am aware that this is a rather rudimentary definition, but it will suffice for our purposes here before a fuller analysis is provided in the next chapter). It is another step, however, to say that Molly's concern is for the other (in this case Sally) rather than for herself alone. Even if we assume that it is Sally's suffering which has occasioned Molly's empathy, Molly's response to her empathy may be to seek to relieve her own discomfort rather than the suffering of Sally. That is, Molly's empathy may direct her away from Sally rather than closer to her. It remains a further question, therefore, how empathy is being directed and employed, and whether this is to moral, non-moral or even immoral ends. To be considered a moral disposition, empathy must be directed to the concerns of others rather than just to oneself. Furthermore, and more specifically, to be a morally worthwhile disposition, empathy must not only be directed towards others but must be done so in a morally positive way.

Something similar, though slightly different, can be said of sympathy – another emotion that is associated with compassion (and again which is explored in more detail in Chap. 3). As it is generally understood, sympathy is not in and of itself a moral concept. To say that Bill feels sympathy for Richard gives us an indication of the emotional sentiment of Bill for Richard, but it tells us very little about the actual plight of Richard (or indeed the moral worth of Bill). As Comte-Sponville (2003, p. 105; emphasis added) suggests, 'what we are sympathising *with* still needs to be taken into account.' Bill may well feel sympathy for Richard, but if that sympathy is motivated by a shared sense of hatred or envy (or some similar vice) or the sympathy is stimulated by Richard's failure to successfully rob a bank, than sympathy in this case is hardly of the morally good kind. As with empathy, to be considered a moral disposition, sympathy must also be directed to the concerns of others in a morally positive way – something which requires more than an emotional response.

What, then, is involved in a broader conception of compassion that involves, but moves beyond, emotions? In her work on pity and compassion Leah Bradshaw (2008, p. 182; original emphasis) contends that 'even if we feel pity for someone, there is nothing virtuous about *feeling* bad about their situation. For compassion to have any substance politically, it has to be converted to virtue, which is measured by reasoned actions'. The connection Bradshaw draws here between thinking and reasoned action is crucial to any conception of compassion as a virtue, and moves compassion from a feeling to also involving reasoned action. While a given emotional response – let us say one of sympathy – *may* lead to other important characteristics of compassion, it equally *may not*. One can imagine a situation in which someone feels sympathy as a result of seeing someone's suffering, but lacks the requisite moral reasoning to arrive at – or at least to further deliberate on – a sound judgement about key aspects of the situation (what has caused the suffering, the level of suffering involved, and what one may or may not be able to appropriately do to relieve the suffering, for example).

There appear, then, to be two particular aspects of compassion which are vital to it comprising a virtue. First, that compassion involves some form of deliberation and discernment, or *practical wisdom*, which involves agents in perceiving the pertinent features of a given situation in a way which informs, shapes and guides both emotional and action-based responses. This deliberation is central to our understanding of compassion as a virtue. Second, that compassion is other-regarding in a positive, and morally worthwhile, way. Central to this second aspect is a sense of *common humanity* that includes a recognition of human fragility, and is based on notions of solidarity and reciprocity. To understand compassion as a virtue, then, we need to explore these two aspects in turn.

PRACTICAL WISDOM

To be compassionate necessarily requires reasoning of some form (Snow 1991; Nussbaum 2001). In her influential work, Martha Nussbaum has referred to compassion as either 'the basic social emotion' (1996, p. 1) or as an 'intelligent emotion' 'occasioned by the awareness of another person's suffering' (2001, p. 301). Similarly, a number of others have also presented compassion as involving a combination of emotion and reason (see, for example, Cassell 2002; Crisp 2008). It is, in part, this relationship between emotion and reason which prevents compassion from falling into sentimentalism.

How, then, might we begin to understand the place of reason within compassion. One way – and indeed a crucial way given my supposition that compassion is best understood as a virtue – is to conceive of reason in Aristotelian terms, and as involving *phronesis*, or practical wisdom. The principle of practical wisdom is central to any Aristotelian informed, agent-centred and context-sensitive understanding of virtue, and Aristotle (2009, pp. 106–107; 1140b) defines practical wisdom as 'a reasoned and true state of capacity to act with regard to human goods'. Central to practical wisdom is both the desire and the judgement necessary to do the right thing. It is through practical wisdom that the moral agent is able to develop the moral perception needed for enacting the virtues – in our case compassion. We should remember, however, that arriving at practical wisdom is a challenge, and cannot be taught in a way divorced from experience. As such, the development of virtues and the practical wisdom necessary for their enactment requires development through practice and habituation. Aristotle (2009, p. 23; 1103a-b) draws the following distinction between natural attributes and learning virtue to explain this:

of all the things that come to us by nature we first acquire the potentiality and later exhibit the activity (this is plain in the case of the senses; for it was not by often seeing or often hearing that we got these senses, but on the contrary we had them before we used them, and did not come to have them by using them); but the virtues we get first by exercising them, as also happens in the case of the arts as well. For the things we have to learn before we can do them, we learn by doing them, e.g. men become builders by building and lyre-players by playing the lyre; so too we become just by doing just acts, temperate by doing temperate acts, brave by doing brave acts.

The moral perception central to practical wisdom involves the capacity to deliberate well about both general and specific situations, to arrive at a decision about an appropriate response, and then, as a result, to enact that appropriate response. It is through practical wisdom that agents are able to evaluate available options in order to discern appropriate and correct choices regarding their emotional and practical responses.

The role of deliberation and discernment – which often involves discerning a course of action when virtues conflict – was illustrated in relation to compassion in a recent BBC (2016) documentary on the US evacuation of Saigon (known as Operation Frequent Wind) in April 1975, in which two ex-US servicemen – Richard Armitage, then a Special Forces Advisor, and Paul Jacob, Captain of the USS Kirk – reflected on their thoughts and decisions to help South Vietnamese civilians seeking refuge:

RA: We steamed down to Con Son Island and we could see on the radar display that there were a lot of blips...There were dozens of ships. Not just Vietnamese naval ships, but also civilian ships. And they were all totally crammed with...with people.

PJ: There are no words to describe what a ship looks like that holds 200 and it's got 2,000 on it. I don't think anybody really understood the magnitude of it until we looked at what we had got in front of us. It looked like something out of Exodus. Our mission was to help the ships into international waters. But now they had all these people...

RA: The US Government already had a refugee problem with the US Naval ships. This was another 30 or more thousand people to deal with...

PJ: We were up all night talking about it...I am convinced that if we sent them back or took them back, they would have killed them all...Armitage decided to bring them. And he didn't get permission from Washington to do that...

RA: I thought it was a lot easier to beg forgiveness than to get permission. So the decision was made and they all went with us.

In this exchange we hear the ways in which the servicemen drew on a range of considerations in order to decide on a compassionate response, taking in particular features of the situation in order to do so. As Aristotle (2009, p. 30; 1106b) tells us, possessing moral virtues means 'to feel them at the right time, with reference to the right objects, towards the right people, with the right motive, and in the right way' (it should be noted here, and as will become clear, while I am making a case for conceiving compassion as a virtue in an Aristotelian sense, Aristotle himself referred to 'pity' – the term Aristotle used for what today we call compassion – as an emotion rather than a virtue). While the partnership of emotions and reason is crucial in this regard, emotion alone cannot provide the necessary judgement for right action without working in concord with reason.[2] To act on the basis of emotion alone, and without reason, therefore is to act with folly. In this sense 'the virtue guides one to be compassionate according to reason' (Ryan 2010, p. 165).

Crucial to understanding practical wisdom in practice is Aristotle's doctrine of the mean. In this Aristotle presents virtuous action as an intermediate path between excess and deficiency, and it is through their practical wisdom that the virtuous agent navigates this path. Thus, virtue 'is concerned with passions and actions, in which excess is a form of failure and so is defect, while the intermediate is a form of success ... therefore virtue is a kind of mean, since ... it aims at what is intermediate' (Aristotle 2009, p. 30; 1106b). Practical wisdom plays a crucial role, too, in the determination of what constitutes the mean, a process through which the virtuous agent discerns the morally salient aspects of the particular context.

In invoking the idea of acting according to the mean, we have an immediate problem so far as compassion is concerned; namely, what constitutes an excess and deficiency of compassion. For some virtues establishing what might constitute an excess or deficiency is relatively clear. Courage, for example, is the intermediate course between rashness (the excess) and cowardice (the deficiency). Modesty, to cite another example, is the intermediate course between shyness (the excess) and shamelessness (the deficiency). To identify what represents an excess or deficiency of compassion is less straightforward, particularly so far as the excess of compassion is concerned. While callousness would seem an appropriate term for a deficiency, a term for an excess is not as readily available. The sort of term we have in mind would be one that would characterise someone overwhelmed by their feeling and regard for the suffering of others. We might refer to such a person as a 'bleeding heart' or as being overly melancholy (in Lady Macbeth's terms someone who is 'too full o' th' milk of human kindess'), but neither seem to provide the sort of conceptual clarity we would want. We can, though, illustrate what we have in mind with regard to an excess and deficiency of compassion in a little more clarity through drawing on narratives about compassion. Speaking on BBC Radio Four's *Beyond Belief* programme, an aid worker with over 30-years experience working to support others, David Bainbridge (BBC Beyond Belief 2015c) has suggested that

> There are two extremes that we have to be very mindful of. I think one extreme we could become so compassionate, so taken up by the suffering we are encountering that it actually becomes almost debilitating. I think the other extreme though is to become so detached and so cold that we now treat these individuals as statistics in a project proposal or images to put out to the public in a public appeal, and really lose the emotion of that compassion.

In these words we have a sense not only of the detachment and callousness we can associate with a deficiency of compassion, but also of the debilitating effects of compassion's excess.

If we accept that compassion represents a virtue in an Aristotelian sense, we can see that compassion involves the moral perception to enact compassion in the right way, at the right time and for the right reason. Furthermore, what precisely might constitute the right way, the right time and the right reasons will differ according to particular circumstances in any given situation – including some consideration of the character and dispositions of the agent – and must be determined through perception and deliberation. Through the capacity to perceive and deliberate well, the moral agent is able to be compassionate appropriate to the particular situation, avoiding excess and deficiency.

With this in mind, there is a further element of acting in accordance with compassion to which up to this point we have only alluded, and which needs some explicit unpicking given its importance with regard to intermediate action. This is the idea that practical wisdom also plays an important role in determining whether compassion is or is not an appropriate response to a given situation in the first place – what in her Aristotelian account, Nussbaum (2001, p. 306) refers to as the 'cognitive requirements' of compassion. Here, Aristotle's account of pity in his *Rhetoric* (which, again, for our purposes here can be understood as broadly comprising what we today call compassion) illustrates the role of practical wisdom in this regard.

Aristotle suggests that our feelings of pity must be regulated by three considerations. First, the suffering of others must be serious and non-trivial.

It would not, for example, make sense to feel pity for someone who had broken a finger nail or who had suffered the loss of a bedding plant in a sharp frost. Indeed, Aristotle (2012, p. 104; Book II, 8) sets out the 'painful and destructive evils' and 'all such evils due to chance' which befit a compassionate response. He characterises the former as 'death in its various forms, bodily injuries and afflictions, old age, diseases, lack of food', and the latter as 'friendlessness, scarcity of friends (it is a pitiful thing to be torn away from friends and companions), deformity, weakness, mutilation, evil coming from a source from which good ought to have come; and the frequent repetition of such misfortunes' (2012, p. 104; Book II, 8).

Second, pity must be reserved only for those whose suffering is undeserved. This characteristic of being undeserving of the suffering befallen has two elements: (1) that the sufferer holds no blame or responsibility for the suffering, or (2) that the sufferer is somehow responsible, but that the suffering is disproportionate to the level of culpability. Now, in the next section I take issue with the idea that compassion is only for those undeserving of their suffering. However, at this point there is a particular feature of the cognitive requirement involved I wish to underline, one which is highlighted by Nussbaum (2001, p. 315). When we understand that suffering afflicts those who are not to blame for their plights, we 'accept(s) a certain picture of the world, a picture according to which the valuable things are not always safely under a person's own control, but can in some ways be damaged by fortune'. In other words, compassion requires us to recognise humanity's fragility. The third cognitive requirement is that pity must involve a sense of shared possibilities. To be compassionate, we must be able to conceive what it means to suffer and accept that the suffering is something which, given human fragility, we will have experienced or will experience.[3]

These cognitive requirements remind us that compassion asks us to make judgements not only about what compassion is as an intermediate response in the given situation, but also as to whether compassion is an appropriate response at all. For this reason, practical wisdom can be said to operate on two, inter-related levels, so far as compassion is concerned. On one level, the agent must make some form of discerned judgement about whether compassion is appropriate to the given situation. On Aristotle's account, for example, whether the suffering is serious, whether it is undeserved and whether shared possibilities are perceptible. Once these conditions are satisfied, the agent must then make further deliberations in order to arrive at (or at least seek to arrive at) an appropriately compassionate response in line with the doctrine of the mean. This involves us in moving between our general conception of compassion and what would best express this ideal within a particular situation taking the salient features of that situation into account. One need not suggest that *all* of the deliberations involved on this second level are of a moral kind (some will involve non-moral practical matters, for example) in order to see that *at least some* important moral judgements will be involved.

The real world is replete with examples of compassion which highlight not only the importance, difficulties and complexities of practical wisdom, but also the contextual specificities at play. Let us consider here two examples, both of which concern the giving of aid. In April 2015 an earthquake in Nepal killed more than 8000 people, injured more than 21,000 and caused widespread devastation. A large and significant humanitarian aid response followed. A week after the earthquake, UN aid officials criticised the Nepalese government for not doing enough to ensure that relief supplies cleared customs and made their way to where they were most needed. In light of these criticisms, Nepalese Finance Minister Ram Sharan Mahat said the following: 'We have received things like tuna fish and mayonnaise. What good are those things for us? We need grains, salt and sugar' (BBC 2015b). In this case, it would be very difficult to suggest that the sending of products such as tuna fish and mayonnaise owes to a lack of compassion per se. To this extent it seems unhelpful and problematic to regard such instances as being sortable into categories of *compassionate* or *not compassionate*. Rather, such cases provide examples not of a lack in compassion, but of a need for further reflection of the sort with which practical wisdom is concerned. From this viewpoint the relevant question changes from 'was compassion at work at all?' to 'which aspects of compassion were or were not at work, and how might these aspects be better framed in future?'.

A second example illustrates the complexities involved even further. Following the liberation of the Bergen-Belsen concentration camp in April 1945, a British soldier, Lieutenant Colonel Mervin Willett Gonin DSO, reflected on aid products received, writing the following in his diary[4]:

> It was shortly after the British Red Cross arrived . . . that a very large quantity of lipstick arrived. This was not at all what we men wanted, we were screaming for hundreds and thousands of other things and I don't know who asked for lipstick.

One first reading, for Gonin (and many would surely concur) the sending of lipstick appears to present a similar case to the sending of tuna and mayonnaise to Nepal. In other words, a compassionate act, prompted by the recognition of suffering and care for others, but which, in the final analysis, somehow misses its mark through sending lipstick rather than some other product which was needed more. Yet, Gonin continues:

> I wish so much that I could discover who did it, it was an action of genius, sheer unadulterated brilliance. I believe nothing did more for those inter-nees than the lipstick . . . At last someone had done something to make them humans again, they were someone, no longer merely the number tattooed on the arm . . . That lipstick started to give them back their humanity.

In this case we are not aware of the thought processes of those sending the lipstick nor directly of those receiving them, but can see the way in which compassionate action was conceived and crucially reconceived as additional salient features of the situation became known.

Examples such as these highlight that being compassionate is not a passive or static endeavour, but is instead an active and dynamic process requiring constant (re)negotiation of our internalised dispositions. Being compassionate – and indeed learning to be compassionate – thus requires that we deliberate within ourselves and with others, including – where possible – about how others have perceived, received and responded to compassionate acts. This involves a recognition that social contexts, which consistently change and adapt over time, shape our experiences and as a result our internalised dispositions. In this way there is an interplay between our character traits and dispositions and the contexts within which we conduct our lives.

In summary of this section, the main intention has been to begin to explore ways in which compassion can be understood as a virtue and, as such, as involving more than an emotional response. To this end, it has been suggested that compassionate agents are compassionate agents to a large extent because they seek to pursue a course of action between excesses and deficiency, guided and mediated by practical wisdom. Given that emotions represent a fundamental element of compassion, something further needs to be said about the relationship between reason and emotions before we conclude. On one reading reason could be viewed – as it was for Plato – as regulating the emotions in the sense of disciplining them or bringing them into line. On another reading, one found in certain readings of Aristotle, reasons and emotions are viewed as working in tandem, or 'sympathy' (Solokon 2006, p. 11). For Aristotle, emotions 'are or should be ideally imbued with reason, rather than controlled by reason' (Kristjánsson 2007, p. 27). Acting virtuously is a matter of both reasoning well in the particular contexts in which we find ourselves *and* responding in an emotionally appropriate way. Through this relationship we can come to experience and enact the emotions in the right way and for the right reasons; through, that is, a 'partnership or concord between reason and emotion' (Solokon 2006, p. 11).

Finally, and to bring this section to a close, I wish to say something briefly here about the education of practical wisdom, though I return to this in more detail in Chap. 6. As the comments I have offered in this section highlight, the development of practical wisdom is not a straight-forward task. What precisely constitutes the right action, for the right reason, at the right time will depend on a variety of agent and situation-specific considerations in relation to our generalised conception of the good life. In part for this reason, the development of *phronesis* is undoubt-edly complex and prohibits simplistic and stable linear trajectories. As Kristjánsson (2015, p. 15; emphasis in original) reminds us, 'becoming more virtuous in a given sphere does not mean taking on virtue wholesale but, rather, gradually moving closer to an *ideal*'. This means that while children may not be able to reach a fully virtuous state and develop *phronesis* in the fullest sense, they are able to move towards virtue and the practical wisdom necessary for it (Sanderse 2015; Kristjánsson 2015). As Sherman (1989, p. 16) argues, from this perspective children occupy a position in which they are 'in progress toward full humanity'. As sug-gested, more will be said about this in Chap. 6.

COMMON HUMANITY

In his 'Beyond Vietnam' speech made in the context of the US military action in Vietnam, Martin Luther King (1964) offered the following reflection:

> as I ponder the madness of Vietnam and search within myself for ways to understand and respond in compassion, my mind goes constantly to the people of that peninsula. I speak now not of the soldiers of each side, not of the ideologies of the Liberation Front, not of the junta in Saigon, but simply of the people who have been living under the curse of war for almost three continuous decades now. I think of them, too, because it is clear to me that

there will be no meaningful solution there until some attempt is made to know them and hear their broken cries.

This powerful extract reminds us that at the heart of compassion is a regard for others. This regard has a number of features, but two, related features in particular are crucial. Integral to compassion is a recognition and concern that *other human beings are suffering*. On one level, this seems a rather trivial statement given its centrality to the very definition of compassion. Yet, there is something deeper that needs to be said about this recognition of common humanity. That is, compassion seems important not only because other humans are suffering, but *precisely because other humans are suffering* – not friends, relations, colleagues or peers, but *humans*. It is the suffering of others and our affinity to them as suffering human beings that renders compassion meaningful. As Comte-Sponville (2003, p. 115) argues, 'compassion . . . makes sense only among equals, or better yet, it realizes this equality between the suffering person and the person next to him, who becomes his equal by sharing his suffering'. In addition, compassion also involves an appreciation that, because of this suffering, the sufferer/s' opportunities for living a flourishing life are being – temporarily or permanently – restricted. By focusing on conceptions of human flourishing, the moral depth required for compassion and compassionate relationships becomes paramount. Compassion is not simply about doing good acts (though of course these are important), but is concerned with relationships built on valuing human flourishing – flourishing which is constrained where suffering is involved. As Nussbaum (2001, p. 310) remarks, 'compassion, or its absence, depends upon the judgments about flourishing the spectator forms; and these will be only as reliable as is the spectator's general moral outlook.' In other words, if we do not value the human possibilities, potential and flourishing of those suffering – if we take some pleasure from or, more commonly, are indifferent to the suffering of others – compassion will fail. Compassion requires, therefore, what Nussbaum terms *eudaimonistic judgements*.

It is these shared features and possibilities for flourishing, based on common humanity, which enable us to be compassionate both to those we know as well as to those who are strangers to us. We see them, for example, in compassionate responses which seek to challenge the causes of suffering, and which alleviate suffering not only as an end in itself but as a means to enabling (re)new(ed) opportunities for flourishing. Yet, we also see them in situations in which there is no hope of ending the suffering, and where compassionate responses aim to preserve human dignity so far as that may be possible. In short, it does not seem possible to offer an account of compassion which does not place a high priority on the positive idea of common humanity, and one which connects to the recognition of human vulnerability.

Compassion, then, involves a positive conception of humanity, of what it means to be human, and, therefore, of other humans. As Aristotle (2012, p. 104; Book II, 8) suggests, 'in order to feel pity we must also believe in the goodness of at least some people'. When we feel an emotional response to the suffering of others, more is involved than simply taking the feelings of others into account. We would also want to take into account the ideas, goals and conceptions of the good held by others (De Waal 2006) – bringing them into some form of relation with our own. In order to do this, we need to know something more about the relationships between human beings, and the extent to which this shapes and informs the sort of recognition of common humanity needed for compassion. Now, the connectedness between human relationships and action are covered in more detail in Chap. 4, but here it is important to make some initial remarks about how human relationships central to compassion can be conceived.

Of central concern here is the nature of relationships between humans, of which the case of the distant stranger provides a pertinent case in point. Adam Smith ([1759] 2009, p. 158) framed this concern in the following way:

> Let us suppose that the great empire of China, with all its myriad of inhabitants, was suddenly swallowed up by an earthquake, and let us consider how a man of humanity in Europe, who had no sort of connexion with that part of the world, would be affected upon receiving intelligence of this dreadful calamity. He would, I imagine, first of all, express very strongly his sorrow for the misfortune of that unhappy people, he would make many melancholy reflections upon the precariousness of human life, and the vanity of all the labours or man, which could thus be annihilated in a moment...And when all of this fine philosophy was over, when all these humane sentiments had been once fairly expressed, he would pursue his business or his pleasure, take his repose or his diversion, with the same ease and tranquillity, as if no such accident had happened. The most frivolous disaster which could befall himself would occasion a more real disturbance. If he was to lose his little finger tomorrow, he would not sleep tonight; but, provided he never saw them, he will snore with the more profound

security over the ruin of a hundred million of his brethren, and the destruction of that immense multitude seems plainly an object less interesting to him, than this paltry misfortune of his own.

As Smith alludes here, with extending our concern for humanity is not always easy. Distant suffering can be, and often is, 'ignored because it [does] not unsettle the routines of everyday life' (Linklater 2014, p. 72).

One response to the problem posed by Smith is to consider it as an expression of his time and to suggest that owing to a range of globalising processes – not least those concerning social and digital media communication – it is simply impossible to avoid an awareness of suffering elsewhere. But this would seem to miss the point, as the problem Smith identifies seems more forceful than one of simple awareness of suffering. Smith's claim is not that one does not identify with the other, bringing them into what Nussbaum refers to as one's circle of concern when suffering, but that such identification can be somewhat fleeting and can quickly be forgotten in the mist of one's own existence. As Nussbuam (2014, p. 195) reminds us, compassion 'will be felt only towards those things and persons we see as important, and of course most of us most of the time ascribe importance in a very uneven and inconstant way'.

Another, deeper, response has been to draw on Kantian-informed, cosmopolitan notions of duty and responsibility. While a diverse and complex field, there is some overlap between cosmopolitan positions which locate ethical responsibilities between humans as stemming from common humanity. Such positions typically hold that citizens today live in increasingly 'overlapping communities of fate' (Held 2005, p. 1), and that recognising common humanity 'translates ethically into an idea of *shared or common duties toward others* by virtue of this humanity' (Lu 2000, p. 245). Illustrative of this line of thought is David Held's (2010, p. 69) suggestion that humanity represents a single 'moral realm' – and that membership of this realm entails and confers duties on human beings qua human beings.

The form of ethic central to cosmopolitanism includes two distinct, though related, core obligations on citizens. The first is the requirement that citizens be 'aware of, and accountable for, the consequences of actions, direct or indirect, intended or unintended, which may radically restrict or delimit the choices or others' (Held 2010, pp. 70–71). The second is that one should act when the humanity and dignity of others is threatened even if this threat is not of one's own making and wherever in the world others may live. This cosmopolitan ethic has ancient roots in the Cynic Diogenes' assertion, when asked from where he came, that 'I am a citizen of the world [*kosmopolitês*]'. These sorts of cosmopolitan commitment found within political science have been replicated within educational discourse (see, for example, Merry and de Ruyter 2011; Osler and Starkey 2003).

In seeking to avoid the focus on duties that seems to be central to such positions, I would like to suggest that one need not claim that we have special *duties* to others to respond positively to the principle of common humanity. Now, there is not scope nor need here to enter into fine detail about the limitations of duty-based forms of cosmopolitanism. I have considered some of the educational limits of duty-based responses to cosmopolitanism elsewhere (Peterson 2012), and for our purposes here some brief comments will suffice to illustrate a central tension involved in positions that seek to draw duties out of common humanity – namely, the idealism that lies at their heart. The issue here is not the expansion of our moral concern to all of humanity, but rather is precisely the drawing of duties to all of humanity that result. This universalising of duty causes a number of tensions, not least the sheer weight of responsibility that (if we subscribe to such views) now rests on our shoulders. Indeed, even its proponents are aware of the utopianism which lies at the heart of such approaches to cosmopolitan ethics. In advocating cosmopolitan education, for example, Merry and de Ruyter, (2011, p. 3) suggest that 'moral education informed by cosmopolitanism is not for the faint heart. Its demands will seem unrelenting. To help prevent moral educators and their pupils from feeling overwhelmed, they will need to acknowledge that moral cosmopolitanism is an *ideal*'.

It must be pointed out that supporters of duty-based cosmopolitanism frequently offer a rejoinder in the form that, in practice, this simply means that one is expected to do their fair share – whatever that means. Thus, and returning to Merry and de Ruyter (2011, p. 2; emphasis added), we are told in a passage of resonance to compassion that 'at a minimum the struggle against injustice entails that one reduce the suffering of others, *as far as one is able*, irrespective of pre-existing desires or relationships, but also geographical proximity, of those in need of help'. Such responses, however, remain problematic. Not only are they somewhat vague, they also raise further practical questions. Do *all* agents need to do their share or will some given proportion of active agents will suffice? Can an agent who is cash-rich but time-poor pay another agent who is cash-poor but time-rich to undertake their share of responsibility? Not only are the answers to these questions difficult to arrive at, they seem to distract us from our central concern – namely, what does it mean to be human and to relate with other humans, other humans who are suffering?

In his critique of cosmopolitianism, David Miller (2002, p. 81) asserts that within such theories 'there is a gap between our moral assessments of states of affairs and the reasons we have for acting in relation to those states of affairs'. This gap is one which seems to me to be crucial. As I suggested above, the rejection of duties stemming from common humanity does not necessarily entail a rejection of the importance and role of common humanity itself. To use Miller's assessment, we may still make a moral assessment about the value and importance of common humanity but offer different reasons for acting in relation to this state of affair. But of what might such different reasons consist?

To start to answer this question, a return to our direct focus on compassion is useful. In 2015 a letter published in the *Guardian* signed by numerous dignitaries of central European countries (including Poland, Czech Republic, Hungary, Slovakia, Latvia, Bulgaria, Estonia, Romania and Croatia) called for action in response to the humanitarian crisis faced by those fleeing from the Middle East. The letter claims that 'as human beings, we have a *duty* to show compassion and to provide them with assistance' (*The Guardian* 2015b). While in no way wishing to detract from the importance and sincerity of the intentions or the situation, there are important reasons why we might *not* want to refer to compassion as a form of duty.

To speak of compassion as a duty seems to involve some form of compulsion, with this compulsion being among the prime reasons *why* one acted this way at all (as in 'I was doing my duty'). A recent example of this line of thought can be found in the discourse surrounding calls for a greater focus on compassionate care in the UK. In a much publicised critique of compassion as a way of addressing standards of care, Anna Smajdor (2013, pp. 2–3) has argued that

> Most averagely compassionate individuals would expect to be moved by the plight of patients calling for water, languishing in soiled bedding, or dying neglected and confused. If this is true, than compassion might be seen as a safety valve, a way of compelling healthcare staff to intervene if things are slipping or patients are suffering. On this view, those who feel no compulsion to intervene when patients are neglected and dying are dangerous in the health service. And if compassion is the means by which such compulsion can be generated, then compassion is what is required in order to forestall similar situations in future.

However in focusing on duty and compulsion, connections which are deeper and more human seem to be obscured. It is these connections, rather than an appeal to duty, which can be found in this powerful end to the letter from the European dignitaries:

> In the name of our humanity, our principles and values, we call upon the authorities and people of our region to demonstrate practical solidarity towards refugees so that they may find safe haven in our midst and enjoy freedom to choose their own future (*The Guardian* 2015b).

In these words we have an understanding of common humanity concerned with solidarity, care for others, and shared concerns and human goals. The intimation here is that we should be concerned to act because of the sorts of people we are qua human beings, rather than because we are following a particular rule or duty, albeit one understood as deriving out of common humanity. The author C. S. Lewis (1985, p. 100; cited in Bohlin 2005, p. 20) expressed this eloquently in his *Letters to Children*:

> A prefect man would never act from a sense of duty; he'd always want the right thing more than the wrong one. Duty is only a substitute for love (of God and other people), like a crutch, which is the substitute for a leg. Most of us need the crutch at times; but of course its idiotic to use the crutch when our legs (our own loves, tastes, habits etc) can do the journey on their own.

In an essential way, when we care for those who suffer, we are committed to them in ways which tie us to their possibilities for flourishing. As MacDonald (2014, p. 89) reminds us the 'motivation of compassion consists in a desire to alleviate the suffering of some set of persons, not a desire to comply with any particular principles'. Similarly, for Haynes (1998, p. 25; emphasis added), ethical responsibility between humans involves a sense of 'responding ... to the concerns of others, *not out of a sense of duty but out of a feeling of responsive mutuality*'. From this position, moral growth includes processes which are both 'dialogical and relational'. Indeed, if we reflect on what may be the archetypal illustration of compassion – the parable of the Good Samaritan – it is not duty but human relationships and conditions such as love, recognising the suffering of the other and bringing the other into relation with one's oneself which are crucial. In other words, it was not a general rule which guided the Samaritan to act, but good character. The power of the parable derives from the fact that, unlike the priest and the Levite, the Samaritan 'decides that this foreigner, this enemy of his people, is his fellow man'

(Rigoni 2007, p. 18). When compassion is viewed as a virtue the motivation to respond to the suffering of others is, then, provided from the internal desire to act in accordance with virtue.

To understand the fellow-feeling central to compassion we also need to have some grasp of the concept of solidarity, given that it is solidarity with others which seems to be central to the human relationships at the heart of compassion and which is often cited as motivating humanitarian concern for others (Baughan and Fiori 2015). *Solidarity* refers to a unity of common feeling and/or action between individuals and groups with shared interest. When solidarity is concerned, our thoughts and actions are framed to work *with* the other, rather than forcing our actions upon them. In this way, solidarity embeds individuals within collectivities, providing and sustaining mutual support. Core aspects of solidarity include a recognition of shared fate between humans, the existence of similar possibilities and an appreciation that the human condition can be, and often is, a fragile one. For these reasons, solidarity brings people closer together, stemming from and building common interests, shared concerns and mutual understanding. As Arnot et al. (2009, p. 253) suggest, the 'source of compassion is not merely in *me* but also in the sense of community, in the sense of shared humanity'. Moreover, solidarity involves a recognition of reciprocity, and as such is concerned with the interconnections and mutual exchange from engaging with others. So far as compassion is concerned, this entails a belief that others would reciprocate if the situation was reversed and/or that we would welcome the compassion of others were we to be suffering.

As with any virtue, compassion requires us to bring into focus our own views about what constitutes human goodness, with our actions guided in turn by that conception (Homiak 1981). Capturing the importance of solidarity, and connecting back to our earlier discussion in the previous section, Martha Nussbaum (2001) has identified a *eudaimonistic judgement* as being central to compassion. Through this judgement, the suffering of others comes to be seen as inherently important to the life of the compassionate agent in a way which moves beyond the idea of similar possibilities, which while informing our *eudaimonistic* judgements do not necessarily provide the close moral connections necessary for compassion. As Nussbaum (2001, p. 319) explains, 'she must take that person's ill as affecting her own flourishing. In effect, she must make herself vulnerable in the person of another.' In this way, solidarity includes the idea that we not only recognise the cause of the other, we bring that cause into our own goals. This sentiment is expressed powerfully in the following quotation, often attributed to Aboriginal elder, activist and educator Lilla Watson: 'If you have come here to help me, you are wasting your time. But if you have come because your liberation is bound up with mine, then let us work together.'

A key component of compassion, then, is that when we are moved by the suffering of others this response is likely to be a reaction to the immediate suffering involved. In addition, however, solidarity also involves us making some account of the ways in which the flourishing of the sufferer are compromised *as well as* the way this compromise represents a limitation upon our own flourishing. Compassion, thus, helps us to recognise certain conditions of humanity, including fundamental characteristics of human flourishing, and provides an important mechanism in any aspirations towards just relationships and communities (Linklater 2007a, 2007b).

It is the principle of human identification central to solidarity and Nussbaum's principle of *eudaimonistic judgement* which brings into serious question the Aristotelian condition that compassion be reserved for those whom are undeserving. As considered in the last section, for both Aristotle and Nussbaum a fuller sense of compassion requires that we judge the sufferer to either be non-culpable for the suffering, or that the suffering is disproportionate to the degree of culpability. This means that when suffering can be attributed to the fault of the sufferer we do not (or at least on this reading, should not) feel compassion in the same way as when the suffering meets the criteria of non-desert.

However, this condition of non-desert seems very hard to agree with if we are to take solidarity seriously. In his analysis, Roger Crisp (2008, p. 235) criticises the principle of non-desert for a number of reasons. First, because of the availability of largely empirical observations that there are many examples of compassion being shown for those who may be seen to have been culpable for their own suffering, and, second, because of the rejection of placing such limits on compassion held to be crucial by many faith traditions. Crisp suggests, therefore, that it seems strange to deny, or to criticise, that we can feel compassion for those who bear a strong degree of culpability for their own suffering, such as those who commit crime and are suffering as a result. Denying or criticising compassion in such situations seems to deny the very common humanity which lies at the heart of compassion.

In this regard the plight of the Bali Nine drug smugglers, and in particular of Andrew Chan and Myuran Sukumaran, seems to provide a particular case in point. In April 2005, in receipt of information from the Australian Federal police, Indonesian officials arrested nine Australian citizens on suspicion of smuggling heroin. Later in 2005 the nine were charged with possession and trafficking of heroin, a charge carrying the death penalty if found guilty. At trial in 2006 two of the Bali Nine – Andrew Chan and Myuran Sukumaran – were sentenced to death by firing squad and both were subsequently denied judicial review. In 2015 appeals for presidential clemency and judicial review were unsuccessful, and the Indonesian government announced preparations for both men to be executed. At this time, advocacy for clemency to be shown intensified across a range of parties – including members of the Australian government, former Australian prime ministers, human rights groups and activists, and members of the general public in both Australia and elsewhere. Appeals pointed to a range of features of the case – the inhumanity of the death penalty, the age of the men at the time of their arrest, and their rehabilitation during their time in prison. At the heart of each was an appeal to compassionate humanity. As the Labour Shadow Minister for Foreign Affairs and International Development, Tanya Plibersek, made clear at the time, 'no one is asking that they be released, no one is asking that their sentences be revoked. Simply that they be allowed to continue to live' (Jabour 2015). On the 29th April Andrew Chan and Myuran Sukumaran were executed. Clearly, compassion was shown to Chan and Sukumaran, and by a great number of people.

Now, both Aristotle and Nussbaum accept that we may feel *something* for those who 'deserve' their suffering which may be similar to compassion, but which nevertheless stops short of being compassion itself. Aristotle uses the term *philanthropon*, while Nussbaum (2004) presents this as a non-moral form of fellow-feeling. However, as cases like the Bali Nine illustrate, suggesting that this is either not compassion, or is some other form of fellow-feeling seems both semantic and misjudged, or as Crisp (2008, p. 236) prefers 'unparsimonious and overblown'. It simply seems to be an over-analysis to seek to distinguish what in all respects, other than culpability, is the same concept. In other words, so far as desert is concerned this does not seem to be a morally crucial term in deciding whether one is – or can be – compassionate. We can add a further element to this suggestion too. One need not even consider those suffering to be of good moral character in order to care about them. We care about them precisely because of their personhood and humanity; because they are a human who is suffering, rather than a particular *kind* of human who is suffering (cf. Callan 1988). Solidarity with others in a way which regards their flourishing as significant and as standing in relation to our own is, thus, crucial.

Now, to say that we may genuinely and justifiably feel compassion for those whose suffering results at least in part from their culpable actions does not necessarily mean that we may feel compassion to the same extent and in the same way. There does seem to be something important, that is, in Aristotle's (2012, p. 105; Book II, 8) suggestion that 'most piteous of all is when... the victims are persons of noble character' and that 'whenever they are so, our pity is especially excited, because their innocence, as well as the setting of their misfortunes before our eyes, makes their misfortunes seem closer to ours'. These suggestions give pause for thought, but I find them to be congruent with a position in which compassion can justifiably be felt in situations of clear culpability. I wish to make clear the suggestion being made here is that compassion may admit different levels of response based on the contextually specific morally and non-morally salient features involved. Compassion, that is, informed and shaped by our understanding of the contexts involved. The compassionate person is not ignorant, but rather understands and enacts their compassion in a way mediated by reason. In doing so the compassionate agent is able, therefore, to distinguish between the formation and expression of compassion and the moral character of the person/s by whom their compassion is stimulated. From this position, 'sharing in the suffering of another does not mean that one approves of him or shares whatever good or bad reasons he has for suffering; it means that one refuses to regard any suffering as a matter of indifference or any living being as a thing.... compassion is not concerned with the morality of its objects' (Comte-Sponville 2003, p. 106). We may experience compassion for the innocent in different ways to the compassion we experience for the culpable – but they are both compassion nevertheless.

CONCLUSION – A TRIADIC RELATIONSHIP

We started this chapter by considering the extent to which, while evoking from emotional responses, compassion involves much more than a feeling – involving as it does reason and (which I have said far less about here, but is explored in detail in Chap. 4) some form of action in response to the suffering. This triadic relationship has been identified within philosophical, theological, psychological and sociological literature (see, e.g., Batson 1994; Clark 1997; Lilius et al. 2011). In their psychological account, for example, Goetz et al. (2010, p. 351) define compassion as 'a feeling that arises in witnessing another's suffering and that motivates a subsequent desire to help'. Through understanding compassion in this way, compassion can be seen as tied to our hearts and heads, and in doing so, stimulates, informs, shapes and mediates our compassionate responses.

The mutually informing and sustaining triadic relationship which comprises compassion involves being exposed to the distress of another (cognitive), being moved by this exposure (affective), and taking action to address or remove the suffering of the other (volitional) (Davies 2010) in ways which involve common humanity and *eudaimonsitic* judgements. In this sense, and for example, the affective dimension of compassion is informed and mediated by reason and in turn motivates the desire for action. Recognising that both are informed by reason, the purpose of the next two chapters is to explore, in turn, compassion's emotions and the forms of action which may comprise compassionate responses.

NOTES

1. I understand that here I am using empathy as referring to an emotional response and, in doing so, am underplaying the cognitive aspects involved in empathy (these are discussed in detail in Chap. 3). However, I think that the point I am seeking to draw here holds in relation to the affective elements on empathy.
2. Some commentators identify a slightly different relationship between reason and emotion in Aristotle. Homiak (1981, p. 634) for example suggests that in virtuous action, 'emotions play a secondary role'.
3. In Emile Rousseau (1762/1979, p. 222) makes something of a similar point when he argues that 'men are not naturally kings, or lords, or courtiers, or rich men. All are born naked and poor; all are subject to the miseries of life, to sorrows, ills, needs, and pains of every kind. Finally, all are condemned to death. This is what truly belongs to man'. Establishing the need for Émile to come into relation with the suffering of others when an adolescent, he continues that 'when the first development of his senses lights the fire of imagination, he begins to feel himself in his fellows, to be moved by their complaints and to suffer from their pains. It is then that the sad picture of suffering humanity ought to bring to his heart the first tenderness it has ever experienced'.
4. http://www.bergenbelsen.co.uk/pages/Database/ReliefStaffAccount.asp?HeroesID=17&

CHAPTER 3

Emotions at the Heart of Compassion

Emotions are central to – and for – compassion, and in the last chapter it was noted that compassion can be viewed as a virtue which stems from an emotional response to the suffering of others. As discussed in Chap. 2, so far as compassion is concerned, emotions play a crucial role in helping us to understand significant moral features of given situations. Thus, for virtues such as compassion, 'the assumption is that without emotions, the moral enterprise would never have gotten off the ground in the first place' (Kristjánsson 2014, p. 348). At this stage of the analysis of compassion offered here, then, it is both necessary and important to engage with precisely what the key emotional aspects of compassion are.

The focus in this chapter is on three particular emotions which have been viewed as central to compassion – in particular, *pity, sympathy* and *empathy* (something is also said about anger, but I take anger to stand in different relation to compassion, as will be explained in the final section of this chapter). In focusing on pity, sympathy and empathy, some may suggest that there are many other emotional states which are important for understanding compassion, such as love or kindness. This may well be so, and I hope to make at least implicit comments about the importance of a range of emotions throughout this book, but there are some good reasons for focusing this exploration on pity, sympathy and empathy.

Not least, all three are consistently (and, as we shall see, not always positively) related to compassion across writing in the field – often in complex and contested ways. As Nussbaum (2001, p.301) reflects, pity,

© The Author(s) 2017
A. Peterson, *Compassion and Education*,
DOI 10.1057/978-1-137-54838-2_3

sympathy and empathy 'appear in texts and in common usage, usually without clear distinction either from one another or from ... compassion'. Yet, each of these concepts seems vital in understanding compassion. In other words, to understand compassion we have to understand not only how pity, sympathy and empathy can and should be perceived, but also how they relate to compassion itself.

The purpose of this chapter, therefore, is to explore the similarities and differences between three emotional responses central to compassion – pity, sympathy and empathy. In framing the analysis offered, I broadly agree with Snow's (1991, p.195) contention that pity, sympathy and compassion (and to some extent I would add empathy here) are best approached as 'members of a small family, related to each other by a few resemblances'.[1] My reason for stating only broad agreement is that I would wish to add, or at least make more explicit, three further points to Snow's which will be explored in this chapter. First, that the resemblances between the concepts are crucial and fundamental to understanding compassion. Second, that this importance stems from the idea that pity, sympathy and empathy are *prerequisites for* compassion. And, third, that this second claim rests not only on the importance of pity, sympathy and empathy, but on the importance of *particular forms* of pity, sympathy and empathy.

Indeed, this third point is of particular significance given the contested conceptual ground involved. As will be explored in the following section, pity, for example, has been given something of a rough treatment within the literature, coming to be viewed in largely negative terms (Nussbaum 2001, e.g., avoids using the term for this precise reason). How we understand key emotional concepts such as pity becomes crucial for those who, like myself, would wish to defend some form of pity in relation to compassion. Indeed, there is a significant tension involved in pity being drawn in overly narrow terms, and being rejected on that basis. In this chapter, then, I wish to examine different ways of perceiving pity, sympathy and empathy. This is the difference between us asking 'are pity, sympathy and empathy morally positive states so far as compassion is concerned?' and 'what *forms* of pity, sympathy and empathy are morally positive capacities, and which are not, so far as compassion is concerned?'. It is the latter question which seems to be of most interest and use to our understanding of compassion, and so the chapter will proceed on this basis.

If more evidence is required of the need for greater conceptual awareness along these lines, we can point to a recent video produced for the Royal Society for the Enlightenment of the Arts (RSA) (at the time of writing the video has been viewed over 6,000,000 times on YouTube) based on Brené Brown's delineation between empathy and sympathy in which the former is advocated over the latter.[2] In the video Brown claims that while 'empathy fuels connections' between people, 'sympathy drives disconnection'. On this basis, Brown conceives sympathy as an unhelpful response to the suffering of others in which those feeling sympathy seek to 'silver line' (and here Brown turns the term 'silver lining' into a verb) the predicament the sufferer is in. This is explained through example exchanges which stem from the suggestion that sympathetic responses begin with 'at least'. For instance:

> 'I think my marriage is falling apart'
> 'At least you have a marriage'

And:

> 'John's getting kicked out of school'
> 'At least Sarah is a straight A student'

In contrast, the empathic response – portrayed as the preferable response – to difficult situations is given as being:

> 'I don't even know what to say right now, I am just so glad you told me'

Now, this may make for an entertaining video, and Brown's thoughts on empathy are insightful, but I am not convinced of the validity of characterising sympathy in such unsympathetic terms. Again, what is at stake here is not whether sympathy is a useful term or not, but rather what forms of sympathy are and are not useful. Understanding the nuances and complexities associated with the second approach, and avoiding the stark dichotomies of the first, seems more productive for our purposes of understanding compassion. Indeed, if we were to draw overly sharp conceptual lines around terms such as pity and sympathy, and accept or reject them on that basis, we are in danger of throwing the baby out with the bathwater.

Furthermore, stating that terms such as pity and sympathy may admit forms which are useful for compassion necessarily brings into focus forms of each which are *less useful* and should be rejected on that basis. This points to a potential fatal problem for compassion – one which any advocate of compassion must tackle head on and which is engaged with throughout this chapter and the two which follow. This is the idea that rather than bringing humans together in equal and mutually reinforcing relationships, compassion is actually inimical to human solidarity and flourishing and is too insecure a basis for morality. That is, rather than alleviating suffering and the causes of suffering, compassion serves to further entrench injustice through (1) entrenching inequalities, (2) increasingly powerlessness and (3) generating compassion fatigue through its consistent and persistent claims on us (this third factor is explored in Chap. 4). On this basis many critics have felt compelled to reject compassion as a viable and positive virtue for democratic life.[3] Indeed, even some of those who support some particular form of compassion have argued that such forms should 'move away from any association with patronage, charity, benevolence, and the like' (Whitebrook 2014, p. 22).

This chapter is divided into four sections. The first three deal respectively with pity, sympathy and empathy, examining different conceptions of each and advancing ways in which each should be viewed as required for compassion. The final section pays brief attention to two other emotions – guilt and anger – in relation to compassion, though both are understood as being secondary emotions to pity, sympathy and empathy as they relate specifically to compassion.

PITY

A number of contemporary debates concerning the nature of compassion have centred on its relationship to 'pity'. In broad terms, we can understand pity as referring to a feeling of recognition and sorrow in response to the suffering of others. However, pity remains a heavily contested and disputed term. A good deal of the conceptual blur from which pity suffers owes to its various uses, and subsequent interpretations thereof, within the history of philosophic thought. We saw in the last chapter, for example, that Aristotle used the term pity for what we would today broadly understand as compassion. Similarly, Rousseau (1755/1994, p. 17) wrote of the importance for social life of man's 'natural repugnance to seeing any sentient beings, especially our fellow human beings suffer', and employed the term *pitié* to refer to a capacity we would, again, broadly understand as compassion. For Rousseau (1755/1994, p. 46), *pitié* involves empathising with those suffering, and it is because of *pitié* that we act in 'aid of those who we see suffering'.[4] A key constituent of *pitié* for Rousseau is the capacity to identify with those suffering, recognising their plight. In *Èmile*, Rousseau (1762/1979, pp. 222–223) suggests:

> To become sensitive and pitying, the child must know that there are beings like him who suffer what he has suffered, who feel the pains he has felt, and that there are others whom he ought to conceive of as able to feel them too. In fact, how do we let ourselves be moved by pity if not by transporting ourselves outside of ourselves and identifying with the suffering animal, by leaving… our own being to take on his being? We suffer only as much as we judge that it suffers. It is not in ourselves, it is in him that we suffer. Thus, no one becomes sensitive until his imagination is animated and begins to transport him out of himself.

At the time Rousseau wrote, the general usage of pity did not carry the negative connotations it possesses today (Nussbaum 2001). For Rousseau, *pitié* involved relationships grounded not in superiority, but in 'a friend's affection' (1762/1979, p. 234). In Rousseau's account of *pitié* within *Èmile*, however, we are introduced to a certain feature of *pitié* which is less edifying and which starts to shed light on some of the negative associations pity holds today. This is the view that in identifying with the suffering of others we derive some form of pleasure from knowing that it is precisely *not* us who is suffering, thereby placing a distance between ourselves and the sufferer (Boyd 2004). Thus, according to Rousseau (1762/1979, p. 221) 'pity is sweet because, in putting ourselves in the place of the one who suffers, we nevertheless feel the pleasure of not suffering as he does'. Partly for this reason some (see, e.g., Boyd 2004) view that *pitié* is presented by Rousseau as principally necessary for *Èmile's* moral development rather than being primarily concerned with alleviating the suffering of others (a more detailed discussion of self-interest in Rousseau's account of self-interest is offered in Chap. 5).

More commonly, pity has been critiqued for other reasons. On many modern readings, pity is a largely negative (or at least largely unproductive) response to the suffering of others, in contrast to the more positive and potentially productive response of compassion. To begin to understand the negative associations of pity today, it is instructive to introduce these criticisms in relation to Aristotle and his doctrine of the mean. According to Kristjánsson (2014, p. 344; original emphasis), what we today call pity (i.e. a recognition in response to the suffering of others) can be understood as an *excessive* form of compassion, involving a deviation, that is, from the intermediate state of the compassionate mean. On this reading, pity involves one feeling distress for those whose suffering is of their own making (which as we saw in the previous chapter, is not included in Aristotle's own account or in some leading accounts that are Aristotelian in nature, such as Nussbaum's).

More typically, however and as Kristjánsson (2014, p. 244; original emphasis) also suggests, most contemporary criticisms of the term generally perceive pity as a '*deficient* form of compassion'. That pity is a deficient form of compassion is illustrated in the following distinction between compassion and pity drawn by Aaron Ben-Ze'Ev who argues that

> compassion involves far greater commitment to substantial help. Compassion involves a willingness to become personally involved, while pity usually does not. Pity is more spectator-like than compassion; we can pity people while maintaining a safe emotional distance from them. While pity involves the belief in the inferiority of the object, compassion assumes the equality in common humanity. (Ben-Ze'Ev 2000, p. 328; see also Whitebrook 2014).

Crucial here are three facets which are understood to distinguish pity from compassion. First, that pity is detached and involves a distancing between the subject and the object of their pity (Boltanski 1999). In this way, pity is viewed as increasing difference between object and subject, deepening rather than reducing the distance between them, and disrupting the bonds of common humanity between the object and subject. Second, that pity does not motivate action in response to the suffering of others, and leads to a lack of urgency on behalf of the pitier (Snow 1991). That is, when one pities the other, and related to the distancing involved, the compulsion to act does not seem so central as is the case when we are truly compassionate. Third, that pity is based on the subject's superiority over the suffering object. Here, for example, Snow (1991) identifies pity as both patronising and dehumanising for the extent to which the pitier conceives that they would either not be in such a position in the first place or, if they were, would not react in the same way (they would, e.g., bear the suffering in a more stoic way or would take greater and more effective steps to end the suffering).

So, given these criticisms of pity – is the concept a helpful one for understanding compassion? There appear to me to be two possible ways in which this might be so. The first is perhaps a somewhat negative way of understanding pity's value in relation to compassion. On this reading pity – at least of the detached, passive and condescending kind – plays a useful conceptual job in understanding what compassion *is not*, and therefore plays some sort of role in helping us what compassion *might be*. That is, if we understand pity to be (1) distanced, (2) passive and (3) involving superior power relations, then we might better conceive compassion as (1) engaged, (2) active and (3) involving equitable relationships between humans. There is something useful to our conceptual task in this way of thinking, and certainly any meaningful and morally salient understanding of compassion would want to aim at the second set of features and not the first. Yet, there is something further about pity which seems to be instructive for compassion.

A second possible way of conceiving the value of pity begins from a recognition that pity represents an important and positive recognition of, and sorrow at, the suffering of others. According to Kristjánsson (2014, p. 344), 'demonizing pity as vice . . . is somehow counter-intuitive; underlying pity is, after all, a fellow-feeling of pain at another person's bad fortune, and fellow-feelings of that sort are generally considered to belong to the province of virtue'. In his 'mitigated defence of pity', Kristjánsson (2014, p. 358) identifies two ways that pity could be a positive, morally justifiable response. Here, recourse to an example of a prisoner suffering as a result of their own culpable action is helpful in delineating the first difference. Contra to Aristotle's belief that the correct response in this situation is one of satisfied indignation rather than pity, Kristjánsson (2014) suggests that there may be certain situations in which we know far more of the nuances of the situation and that, as such, we 'will need to take many other considerations into account, which means that . . . the eventual recommendation elicited by our *phronesis* could well be: feel pity'.

To understand Kristjánsson's second defence of pity we must recall his suggestion that, for Aristotle and in line with the doctrine of the mean, pity can be understood as an excess of compassion. In line with this standpoint, Kristjánsson (2014, p. 359) invokes the idea that people will have a tendency to 'err on the side of one, rather than the other, extreme of a virtue'. As a result, there are times when it is necessary to focus on the other extreme. The suggestion here is that in a context in which it is more likely that people will err on the deficient side of compassion (i.e. callousness), there may be good reason to 'intermittently' feel pity 'in order to strengthen compassion' (359). In this sense, pity can play an important role in counter-balancing less positive responses such as callousness.

Kristjánsson's position on pity, builds from, and extends, Eamonn Callan's work on the concept. In response to criticisms of pity, Eamonn Callan (1988, p. 1) asks how we would regard someone without pity, suggesting that 'if I had a pitiless heart my entire life would surely be an abject moral failure'. As a result, we seem to be in something of a paradoxical situation in which 'a pitiless heart may be a terrible thing, but a fondness for dispensing pity is scarcely any better'. While Callan (1988, p. 4) accepts that pity can be of the 'contemptuous' kind, he contends that pity involves, and is stimulated by, a basic respect of, and care for, personhood. As Callan (1988, p. 10) explains,

> Given that one cares for others as persons and believes that autonomy is essential to the dignity of persons, one is necessarily prone to feel sorrow on their behalf when others are trapped in pathetic situations.

That is, at the heart of pity *is* a spontaneous recognition of others' suffering which prompts a sense of caring for those who are suffering, and a sense of sorrow based on recognition of personhood and common humanity – which while it may become corrupted by condescension, does not necessarily have to be. It is this caring for others which provides an important salient reason why we would regard an absence of pity as morally problematic, and it is when this concern for others takes on a contemptuous nature that we find pity unpalatable.

Pity, then, is a problematic concept given that some – we might even say currently dominant – readings of it invoke relationships antithetical to compassion. My concern here has not been to dismiss criticisms of this form of pity. Rather it has been to suggest that these are not the only readings of pity available to us, and that there remains a kernel at the heart of pity which remains important, and which speaks of the humanity central to compassion, namely the recognition that another is suffering and a sorrow at this suffering. Yet – and fairly obviously – pity does not do all of the work necessary for compassion. Pity does not necessarily help us to identify fully with others who are suffering (which it was suggested is fundamental to conceiving compassion as a virtue in the previous chapter), and nor does it – alone – provide a motivation to alleviate the suffering of others. We need, therefore, further concepts through which to understand and appreciate how we might move from this recognition toward compassion. A key concept in this regard is sympathy, and it is to sympathy that we will now turn.

SYMPATHY

On a surface level, sympathy and pity are very similar. Like pity, a broad definition of sympathy also views it as involving a *recognition and sorrow* that the other is suffering. Because they are both concerned more generally with *misfortunes*, both pity and sympathy take account of a wider range of events, instances and conditions than compassion – ranging from the fairly trivial to the catastrophic (Snow 1991). As we look more closely, however, an important difference – one highly relevant to compassion – between sympathy and pity can be drawn. On most readings, sympathy is understood as involving a closer moral and relational connection between humans than might be the case with pity (and certainly as is the case with condescending forms of pity). According to Garber (2004, p. 23) sympathy is 'historically a condition of equality or affinity', and as David Konstan (2014, p. 181; emphasis added) remarks, 'sympathy in the modern construal of the term involves *identification* with another', and it is this identification not only with the other, but with the other *suffering from misfortune*, that is important to our understanding of compassion. It is in identifying with others that we start to draw them closer to our circle of concern, reducing the distance between ourselves and others, and through which we also start to consider their human possibilities in relation to our own.

As we explored in the previous chapter, the reduction in distancing is fundamental to a morally relevant conception of compassion, and here the shared sense of personhood and human fragility are again crucial. To this end, sympathy plays an important role in compassion. Concerned as it is with a deeper feeling of sorrow occasioned by the suffering of others than is the case with pity, sympathy requires us to come in to some form of relation with others at a human level based on an identification with them – though at a more general level than that required by compassion. Often cited in this regard is the following passage from Rousseau's (1762/1979, p. 224) *Émile* in which this recognition of common humanity and human fragility is central:

> Why are kings without pity for their subjects? Because they count on never being mere men. Why are the rich so hard toward the poor? It is because they have no fear of becoming poor. Why does the nobility have so great a contempt for the people? It is because a noble will never will be a commoner. Why are the Turks generally more humane and more hospitable than

we are? It is because, with their totally arbitrary government, which renders the greatness and the fortune of individuals always precarious and unsteady, they do not regard abasement and poverty as a condition alien to them. Each may be tomorrow what the one whom he helps is today.

For this reason, Rousseau advises:

> Do not, therefore, accustom your pupil to regard the sufferings of the unfortunate and the labors of the poor from the height of his glory; and do not hope to teach him to pity[5] them if he considers them alien to him. Make him understand well that the fate of these unhappy people can be his, that all of their ills are there in the ground beneath his feet, that countless unforeseen and inevitable events can plunge him into them from one moment to the next. (1762/1979, p. 224)

I wish, then, to make the following claims about sympathy. First, that while similar to pity, sympathy represents a deeper form of engagement with the other in which we *identify* with the other suffering from misfortune on the basis of shared human concerns. Second, and for this reason, sympathy stands in important connection to compassion, given that identification with others is a prerequisite of compassion (we might also note that it simply makes no sense to say that we feel compassion for someone for whom we are unsympathetic!).

But is sympathy useful to our understanding of compassion in other ways? If sympathy is of further use, it would seem to be in relation to its role as a potential motivator for the alleviation of suffering. In other words, when we feel sorrow at the suffering of others with whom we identify, does this feeling motivate us to act to lessen or remove the suffering in a way which – as we have seen – pity does not? Within the literature on sympathy, there is some disagreement about the relationship between sympathy and alleviating action. As we saw in relation to the RSA video on the differences between empathy and sympathy, for example, sympathy has (and wrongly on my account) been viewed as driving disconnections between humans. Now, it seems reasonable to suggest that sympathy *might* motivate the alleviation of suffering, but that equally it *might not*. We may accept, for example, that one could be sympathetic but not take action, particularly in situations where the misfortune is less serious. Imagine a situation in which a worker approaches their boss, explains that they have an ill child who needs collecting from school and taking care of for the rest of the day, and therefore requests permission to take the rest of the day off from work. We can readily imagine that the boss may be sympathetic (they may have children themselves and have been in a similar situation on many occasions), but is not willing to take action. Even in cases where the misfortune is more serious and meets the sorts of requirements for compassion explored in Chap. 2, we can conceive that people can be sympathetic without acting altruistically to alleviate the suffering. Consider, for example, the case of Susan, who watches a news report on her television of peoples fleeing from persecution or suffering the effects of famine, feels a strong sense of sympathy at the suffering of their fellow humans, but switches off the television and takes no action. We can accept that Susan genuinely feels sympathy for those suffering. She identifies with those suffering as fellow human beings whose possibility for flourishing are restricted and feels a deep sorrow at the suffering they are experiencing (note here that the feeling of sorrow may stay with Susan for a time after turning off the television, maybe even days, weeks or longer). That Susan is sympathetic appears to be independent from whether that sympathetic feeling motivates action – it may or it simply may not.

Yet, this is a different claim from saying that sympathy may not be important at all in motivating action. Within the literature, there is a good deal of support for the idea that sympathy *can* help to motivate a desire to alleviate suffering (Sverdlik 2008; Kristjánsson 2014; for some empirical research in psychology which seems to support this view, see Eisenberg 1986). Indeed, there does seem to be some prima facie reasons for thinking that sympathy may be involved in motivating action. When Rachel watches a television news report depicting the suffering of others, and when Rachel sympathises with those suffering as a result, she may well (and unlike Susan) decide upon some course of action that seeks to alleviate this suffering. In such situations, though, there seem to be other important processes involved which interact with sympathy to motivate and guide action. So we would not want to dismiss the motivating role of compassion completely, but rather temper this with the two provisos that sympathy may not necessarily lead to alleviating action and that when it does, it does so in combination with other capacities (of which I will say more in the next section on empathy).

The argument in this section so far has been that sympathy plays a role within compassion in that it (1) helps us to identify with others who are suffering misfortune, (2) involves a feeling of sorrow for that suffering bringing us closer to the sufferer than is the case with pity and (3) also forms *part* of a range of motivating factors which stimulate agents to act to alleviate the suffering of others. Before concluding, however, several further points need to be made which are relevant to our focus on compassion. First, sympathy would seem to have a wider focus than compassion, taking account of misfortunes that are more trivial and less serious than would be the case for compassion. For this reason, as an emotional response to suffering, sympathy would seem to be somewhat independent of further, reasoned conditions. Second, and related to this, it is important to clarify that one of the points I am seeking to make about sympathy is that sympathy *in and of itself* does not take account of the moral worth of either the sympathiser or those who they are sympathising with. This notion was considered in the previous chapter, so I will not repeat this in full here, apart from reiterating that sympathy gains moral worth precisely when it comes into relation with compassion, through which it becomes directed to the concerns of others (in our case here, others who are suffering) in a morally positive way. As Ure (2014, p. 247) concludes, 'if our natural capacity for sympathy is to become a moral compass, it must be informed by a perspective that acknowledges ... human vulnerability.' In other words, there are instances when sympathy has no moral worth (when Geoff feels sympathy for a would-be murderer whose intended victim escapes) and others when quite clearly it does (when Alan feels compassion, and thus has sympathy, for those whose suffering he recognises and identifies with based on principles of common humanity and fragility).

A third important point to consider, and which is helpful in understanding sympathy as a component of compassion, is that sympathy – while bringing the object closer to the subject – still rests on the perception of suffering *held by the sympathiser* rather than the object of sympathy (see, e.g., Nussbaum 2001; Sverdlik 2008). When Rachel sympathises with those whose suffering she has witnessed on a television news report, she is reconstructing their suffering. While important, this does not necessarily take account of precisely how the sufferer is actually feeling and thinking about their situation. Sympathy has the possibility, therefore, of an emotional and psychological gap or misreading. This brings to mind Adam Smith's (1759/ 2009, pp. 16–17) illustration of the gap which can exist in our compassionate reconstructions of others:

> Of all the calamities to which the condition of mortality exposes mankind, the loss of reason appears, to those who have the least spark of humanity, by far the most dreadful, and they behold that last stage of human wretchedness

with deeper commiseration than any other. But the poor wretch, who is in it, laughs and sings perhaps, and is altogether insensible of his own misery. The anguish which humanity feels, therefore, at the sight of such an object, cannot be the reflection of any sentiment of the sufferer. The compassion of the spectator must arise altogether from the consideration of what he himself would feel if he was reduced to the same unhappy situation, and, what perhaps is impossible, was at the same time able to regard it with his present reason and judgment.

Smith's example raises the question of how can we come to acknowledge human vulnerability in a way which strives to bring one's own construction of the suffering of others into relation with the actual feelings, perceptions and understandings of those actually suffering? In other words, how might we seek to close the gap which exists between our constructions and the realities of others? Such an endeavour seems crucial if we accept Blum's (1987, p. 232) contentions that

> expanding our powers of imagination expands our capacity for compassion. And conversely the limits of a person's capacities for imaginative reconstruction set limits on her capacity for compassion.

Taking the need for imaginative reconstruction seriously as a key component of compassion requires that we engage in detail with a third emotional response – *empathy*. In the next section, the emotional and cognitive nature of empathy is examined. I will suggest, first, that empathy plays an important role in bringing the compassionate subject and object closer together, and second, that – mediated by the principle of care – empathy plays a crucial role in motivating compassionate action.

EMPATHY

In Harper Lee's *To Kill a Mockingbird* (1960, p. 33) Atticus Finch advises his daughter, Scout, that 'you never really understand a person until you consider things from his point of view . . . until you climb into his skin and walk around in it'. It is this view – that to understand others we have to imagine ourselves into their position – which commonly, though not completely defines empathy. For this reason, empathic understanding admits a focus which is much broader than pity and sympathy. Generally speaking, we may seek empathic understanding with someone who is happy just as much as we may do so with someone who is in pain.

The same is clearly not true of pity or sympathy. This reminds us that, so far as compassion is concerned and involving as it does the suffering of others, our interest here is not in empathy in its entirety. Rather, our focus is on empathy in regard to situations in which others are suffering.

At its core, empathy can be understood as involving in to repeat Blum's term an *imaginative reconstruction* of the other (their thoughts, experiences, motivations, feelings, for example). It is through this imaginative reconstruction that we come in to relation with, and seek to understand and share, the perspectives of others. In compassion's case, the others with whom we are concerned are those who are suffering, and it is for this reason that empathy has been viewed as comprising part of the 'pathway towards compassion' (Daniel 2013). It is this imaginative reconstruction which is often central in calls for compassion toward others, as the following extract from Martin Luther King's (1964) 'Beyond Vietnam' anti-war speech illustrates:

> Here is the true meaning and value of compassion and nonviolence, when it helps us to see the enemy's point of view, to hear his questions, to know his assessment of ourselves. For from his view we may indeed see the basic weaknesses of our own condition, and if we are mature, we may learn and grow and profit from the wisdom of the brothers who are called the opposition.

Crucial to this imaginative reconstruction is a *sharing in the perspectives of others*, which in turn, can be said to involve two, interrelated dimensions – one affective and one cognitive – both of which are significant for compassion. In her analysis of empathic understanding for fictional characters, Snow (2000, p. 71) suggests that 'cognitively, we at least have to believe that the other is genuinely experiencing emotion. Affectively, it seems that we have to be disposed to care about, or have an interest in, the other's experience'.

I take this sharing of perspectives to be fundamental to understanding empathy, and indeed compassion, and understand the sharing of perspectives in a way which involves an imaginative reconstruction of the other to be *the* defining characteristic of empathy, and that it is this characteristic which directs us to, and informs, the sorts of capacities needed to bring it about (about which I will say more below). However, by understanding empathy in terms of an imaginative reconstruction – or the coming into relation with the perspectives, feelings and goals of others through our imagination – we immediately have an important definitional problem. In a strict sense, perspective-taking can be understood as a process in which one takes the perspective of another or of an alternative position regarding, say, a particular issue. On this strict reading, perspective-taking is presented as a largely (and sometimes wholly) cognitive affair that can be contrasted (though may well be related to) the emotional engagement with which empathy is also concerned. As I am using the term here, and as is often the case in its general usage, I understand sharing the perspectives of others in a wider sense – as involving *both* cognitive and affective dimensions, and as involving the concord of reason and emotion. Indeed, and to repeat, it is this interplay between the cognitive and affective which seems crucial to our understanding of, and engagements in, empathy.

So, if sharing perspectives is concerned with an imaginative reconstruction of the others' cognitive and affective states, what precisely is involved in this imaginative endeavour? While the ability to imagine is a central condition of empathy, how it is conceived is open to a number of interpretations, each of which understands the cognitive and emotional aspects – and the relationship between the two – in particular ways. To try and simplify matters, we can understand empathy to be concerned with an endeavour through which we *either or at the same time* (1) transpose ourselves into the mindset of the (suffering) other and/or (2) imagine how we would think, feel and act if we were suffering in that way. Through empathy we come to engage cognitively and affectively with the condition of the other, and in doing so bring them, their suffering, their ideas, their thoughts and their goals into relation with our own ideas, thoughts and goals. In other words, and as made clear above, while cognitive imagination is a necessary condition of the sort of empathy which compassion needs, it is not sufficient alone without emotion and *vice versa*. Compassion involves an emotional response to the suffering of others which operates in relation with our cognitive endeavours.

We need, though, to say a little more about the precise nature of reconstruction involved, something which becomes particularly important when the affective dimensions of empathy are our focus. Writing in support of developing empathy through Philosophy for Children, for example, Schertz (2007, p. 189), defines affective empathy as being concerned with 'the absorption or assimilation of another's emotional state'. The inference here is that when we empathise with the suffering of others we actually feel what they are suffering. This precise claim is made by

Peters and Calvo (2014, p. 50; emphasis added) who define empathy as 'experiencing *the same emotion* as another'. There seem to be good reasons for suggesting that such claims should be treated with caution. Even were it psychologically possible to feel the same emotional response as another, it is not always clear that this is what is actually going on in cases of empathy. We might say, for example, that we feel some form of emotional distress when others are starving or are suffering physical pain, but it seems a step too far to suggest that the *same emotion* is being experienced by both the sufferer and the empathiser. Even when we say that we feel sad because others are sad, the sort of sadness is *different in kind* from the precise sadness which the other is feeling (and is much better understood as a sorrow relating to fellow-feeling – a form of sympathy – as is traditionally the case with compassion).

A form of empathy which equates to actually feeling what the other feels is qualitatively different from what is usually understood by empathy, and what I take to be its importance for compassion – namely, an imaginative reconstruction of the suffering of others rather than a physical replication and embodiment of that suffering.[6] It is this imaginative reconstruction of other's emotional states which is more commonly found in assessments of empathy, and which is illustrated by White (2008, p. 38; emphasis in the original) when he argues, for example, that 'even though we may never be kings, we *can* imagine what it would be like to be Oedipus and we can identify with the sufferings of Antigone though it is unlikely that we will ever be in her impossible situation'. Again here, the sentiment of Atticus Finch is clear – we only come to understand the other through stepping into their role and imagining their position and feelings.

But what, precisely, does stepping into their role and imagining their position mean so far as feelings are concerned? As suggested previously appear to be two ways in which we can understand the imaginative enterprise central to empathy. First, we can use our imagination to form some conception as to how the victim is feeling (as illustrated by Adam Smith in the case of the person who has lost reason). That is, when John sees Richard suffering, John imaginatively reconstructs how he believes Richard will be feeling. We can imagine, for example, John saying something along the lines of 'I imagine that Richard is feeling agitated, a great deal of physical pain, or upset and, because I care about Richard's wellbeing, I feel sorrow at his current state'. Second, we can picture ourselves in the place of the victim and imagine how we would feel if we were in their position. In this situation, John sees Richard suffering and imagines how he (John) would respond were he to be suffering as Richard is. Here we can imagine John saying something along the lines of 'Because I care about Richard I imagine if I were in Richard's position, I would feel physical pain, agitation and upset, and this occasions me to feel sorrow at his current state.' In the first example, John is imaginatively reconstructing what he takes to be *Richard's* responses. In the second, John is imaginatively reconstructing his *own* response were he to be in Richard's position.

In his account of compassion, Blum (1987, p. 231) makes clear his support only for the first form of imagination reconstruction, arguing that this 'consists in imagining what the other person, given his character, beliefs, and values, is undergoing, rather than what we ourselves would feel in his situation'. It is important to note, however, and contra Blum's account, that these two ways of understanding the imaginative reconstruction are unlikely to operate independently and in isolation. When we empathise, we are engaging with imaginative reconstruction in both forms. Indeed, it would seem likely that John can only imagine Richard's emotional response if he has some conception of how he would respond himself upon which to draw. What remains crucial to both – and this is crucial for compassion – is that empathy focuses 'on the onlooker's point of view, making the best judgement the onlooker can make about what is really happening to the person'. My point here, is that in order to make this judgement, the onlooker will invariably draw on their imaginative assessments of *both* (1) the sufferers' perspectives, feelings and goals and (2) how they would feel were they in the sufferer's shoes.

Understanding empathy in this way moves us beyond seeking some sort of match between the perspectives of others and our own, which are always fallible (more will be said about this later). The focus instead becomes the imaginative processes concerned with seeking to understand the other (their perspectives, feelings and goals etc.) in a way which builds the fellow-feeling necessary for compassion. The psychological work of Martin Hoffman (2000, p. 30; original emphasis) helpfully guides our focus here:

Affective empathy seems like a simple concept – one feels what the other feels – and many writers define it in simple outcome terms: One empathizes to the extent that one's feelings matches the other's feeling. Consequently, I have found it far more useful to define empathy not in terms of outcome (affect match) but in terms of the processes underlying the relationship between the observer's and the model's feelings. The key requirement of an empathic response according to my definition is **the involvement of psychological processes that make a person have feelings that are more congruent with another's situation than with his own situation.**

In his elucidation of these processes Hoffman (2000, pp. 54–58) identifies three ways of conceiving what he refers to as 'role-taking'. First, role-taking is 'self-focused' when we place ourselves in the position of those suffering and consider how we would feel (as in the second example of John and Richard above). Self-focused role-taking in this way can include our drawing on analogous situations from our pasts in order to inform our placing ourselves in the position of others. A second approach is 'other-focused' role-taking. Here the imaginative task concentrates on the feelings of those suffering (as in the first example of Richard and John above). By focusing on the other, we take account of their views, feelings, character and condition in order to inform our perceptions of their suffering. Drawing on empirical studies, Hoffman explains that self-focused role-taking is associated with stronger feelings of emotional distress. In other words, when we imagine how we would feel in the situation of the sufferer our affective concern is stronger than when we imagine what the other is feeling.

However, Hoffman (2000, p. 58) cautions that by focusing too much on the self, there is a danger of 'egoistic drift', through which the empathiser becomes overly absorbed with their own state, rendering a loss of connection with the other. For this reason, Hoffman (2000, p. 58) contends that a third approach, which combines self-focused and other-focused role-taking, is more appropriate to understanding the imaginative relationships involved in empathic distress. This is because,

> it combines the emotional intensity of self-focused role-taking with the more sustained attention to the victim of other-focused role-taking. Indeed, fully mature role-taking might be defined as imagining oneself in the other's place and integrating the resulting empathic affect with one's personal information about the other and one's general knowledge of how people feel in his or her situation. It could go either way: other-focused role-taking in the service of self-focused role-taking, or self-focused role-taking in the service of other-focused role-taking.

I take the combination set out by Hoffman to be both instructive and useful to understanding empathy as a key component of compassion, combining as it does the relationships between self and other as well as that between cognition and affect. Both of these interplays seem fundamental to understanding the relationship between the empathiser and the sufferer, as well as the imaginative endeavour involved.

The main dimensions of empathy thus defined, we still need to say more about empathy's importance for compassion. To do so is to recognise that while imaginative reconstruction may be important for empathy, it may not be sufficient – alone – for compassion. Recent research conducted with those who have suffered from adversity in their own lives, for example, has tentatively suggested that it is 'empathic *concern*' (what I will refer to as empathic distress), rather than perspective-taking per se, which 'predicted the regular emergence of compassion' (Lim and DeSteno 2016, p. 177; emphasis added). It seems, therefore, that there is good reason to say something further about what 'empathic concern' might mean in relation to compassion.

To understand empathic concern in relation to compassion it is instructive to consider the relationship between empathy and what psychologists typically call *helping behaviour* – or what Welp and Brown (2014, p. 55) refer to as the 'empathy-altruism hypothesis' (see also, Eisenberg and Miller 1987; Batson 1991, 1994). In his detailed psychological analysis of empathy, Hoffman (2000) surveys a range of empirical work which posits not only that there is a positive association between empathy and helping behaviours, but that empathic distress *precedes* such helping. That is, empathic distress at the suffering of others motivates us to some form of behaviour aimed at alleviating the suffering. Moreover, such connections have not only been identified in adults, but also as developing throughout childhood and into adolescence (for a review of literature in specific relation to children, see Eisenberg et al. 2006).

Though there is some consternation about the precise measures of empathy and prosocial behaviours involved (for an overview see, e.g., Wilhelm and Bekkers 2010[7]), there does seem to be a body of work which draws positive connections between empathy and the sorts of helping behaviours one would equate with compassion – taking in both 'spontaneous, short-term types of helping' as well as 'planned, long-term types of helping behaviour' (Wilhelm and Bekkers 2010, p. 12; For an alternative reading see Crisp (2008) who dismisses empathy as a prerequisite of compassion[8]). In their analysis, and drawing data from the *General Social Survey* in the US, Wilhelm and Bekkers (2010) interrogate the relationship between dispositional empathy, caring and helping behaviour among adults in order to evaluate three hypotheses which are of relevance to our focus. The first hypothesis is that existing evidence suggests positive associations (1) between dispositional empathy and helping behaviour and (2) between the principle of care and helping behaviour. The second, drawing on the work of Hoffman, is that dispositional empathy is mediated by the principle of care in support of helping behaviour. In this second hypothesis, empathy is understood to work 'through care' to motivate helping behaviour (2010, p. 15). The third hypothesis is that, the principle of care plays a greater role in mediating the association between dispositional empathy and helping behaviour for planned and longer-term actions than it does for spontaneous, shorter-term actions.

Summarising the results of the study, Wilhelm and Bekkers report that while both empathic concern and the principle of care are positively associated with many helping behaviours, this association is more consistent for the principle of care. That is, when the principle of care is removed, the strength of the dispositional empathy-helping behaviour association reduces, but this is not the case for the association of principle of care-helping behaviour when dispositional empathy is partialled out. In relation to the second and third hypotheses, Wilhelm and Bekkers (2010, p. 25) report findings in support of the proposition that dispositional empathy is indeed mediated by care, and that 'the principle of care mediates the empathy-helping relationship more strongly for planned helping behaviour'. That is, while the principle of care is highly important (though not always crucial) in mediating empathy so far as short-termed helping with those in immediate and close proximity, it becomes crucial for planned long-term helping. Such findings suggest that while empathy is central to the forms of helping behaviour one would associate with compassion – both spontaneous, short-term and planned, and long-term – without the mediation of the principle of care its effect is importantly reduced.

Working *together*, then, empathy and the principle of care inform and engender the sorts of helping behaviour required for compassion. In being fundamentally concerned with imagining the other – explained here as involving an interplay between self-focused and other-focused role-taking – empathy helps to connect the compassionate agent to those suffering. When we are involved in imaginative exercises of this kind cognitive and affective distances are reduced in a way which not only brings the other into relationship with us, but – when mediated by the principle of care – does so in a way which evokes, builds and sustains our concern for their suffering.

So far in this section, the core dimensions of empathy have been set out and some fundamental ways empathy connects to compassion have been suggested. It has been argued that a range of factors are important in understanding empathy as a component of compassion – in particular, the closing of the gap between compassionate subject and object brought about through imaginative reconstruction and the relationship between empathic distress and the principle of care. In what is left, I would like to say a little more about the sorts of capacities which might be seen to be central to the combined role-taking necessary for empathy's imaginative project.

First, role-taking of the sort needed for empathy requires an *intellectual and emotional openness*. Of importance here is the capacity to be open-minded and willing to enter into further dialogue with others in order to hear further arguments and contentions, and to revise our understandings, perspectives and feelings on this basis. In his analysis of intellectual virtues, Jason Baehr (2011, pp. 151–152) makes the following points concerning open-mindedness:

> whether a particular instance of cognitive 'detaching' or 'transcending' counts as an instance of open-mindedness depends in part on the immediate motivation behind it. Imagine a person who sets aside or moves beyond one of his beliefs, but who has no real intention of making an honest or fair assessment of this argument… Intuitively, this person is not genuinely open-minded. And the reason, it seems, is that he is not committed to taking seriously the opposing argument. This suggests that where open-mindedness involves assessing one or more competing views, it necessarily involves doing so with the aim of giving these views a 'serious' (fair, honest, objective) hearing or assessment.

Here we have some features which are equally important so far as empathic imagination is concerned. In particular, an honest and genuine openness to enter into cognitive and affective engagement with the other is crucial. That is, we must be sure that we are engaging with others in ways which respect their humanity; because we are genuinely concerned with their suffering and understand imaginative engagement as a way to bring us closer into relation with this suffering rather than serving other ends. Central to empathy, than, are associations rooted in sincerity, mutual concern and unforced dialogue, rather than less positive self-serving ends (though as explored in Chap. 5, this does not necessarily mean that compassion does not involve an element of concern for self).

Being open in this way immediately brings into focus the existence of different conceptions of the good life, particularly if we accept that compassion requires us to widen our circle of concern beyond our immediate relationships. This widening means that when we enter into compassionate relationships with others who hold different conceptions of the good life, we need to recognise and appreciate how others may bring their own ideas of human flourishing into relation with our own. Moreover, it requires us to *listen* to the situation of others, taking into account a range of information (the verbal and non-verbal communication of those suffering, communication from those advocating on their behalf, for instance) which enable us to get closer to others. As Benjamin Barber (1984, p. 179) suggests, 'the skills of listening are as important as the skills of talking', and involve us 'receiving as well as expressing, hearing as well as speaking, and emphasizing as well as uttering'. In this way, empathy can play an important moral role in allowing us to engage with, and to seek to understand, the moral goals and ideas of others – including those concerning what constitutes the good life.

Second, and integrally related to openness, because compassion involves one imaginatively constructing the suffering of another, we must recognise that it is by its very nature limited and fallible. Dewey (1933, p. 9) describes this process as one concerned with the 'active, persistent and careful consideration of any belief or supposed form of knowledge in the light of grounds that support it and further conclusions to which it tends'. Central here is recognising the existence of what might be termed an *imaginative gap* between our (re)construction of the sufferer and their suffering, and the sentiments, beliefs, constructions held by those who are suffering[9] (Nussbaum 2001). If we accept the premise of an imaginative gap, and that such gaps owe to a range of possible contributory factors – including perhaps, ignorance, a lack of imagination, incomplete facts or misunderstanding – it becomes necessary to ask how we might go about closing the gap. I return to this question in Chap. 6 in specific relation to education and the sorts of educational endeavours which may be worthwhile to this end.

COMPASSIONATE ANGER

The concern of this chapter so far has been to explore the feelings and emotions central to compassion; namely, pity, sympathy and empathy. Before concluding the chapter there are, however, other emotional responses which may be seen to relate to compassion in important ways. Of these, anger appears of particular relevance to compassion and therefore will be briefly considered.

Of those affective responses to the suffering of others that stand in addition to pity, sympathy and empathy, it is anger which is most often cited. As it related to compassion, anger is perhaps best understood as a secondary emotion because beyond a superficial level it depends in the first place on the existence of pity, sympathy and empathy. That is, compassionate anger builds from a sorrow at the suffering of others, our care for others, and our imaginative reconstructions of their suffering.

Anger can play something of an important role in motivating the compassionate agent to (seek to) not only alleviate the suffering but to challenge the structural causes of the suffering. Along these lines, Borg (1997, p. 50) argues that compassion

> leads us to see the impact of social structures on people's lives. It leads to seeing that the economic suffering of the poor is not primarily to do with individual failure. It leads to seeing that the categories of 'marginal', 'inferior', and 'out-cast' are human impositions. It leads to *anger* towards the sources of human suffering, whether individual or systemic.

In his analysis of research in social psychology exploring the relationship between compassion and anger and guilt, Faulkner (2014b, p. 107; emphasis in the original) summarises that anger is likely to be more effective than guilt in motivating compassionate helping, because

> while guilt tends to increase individuals' support for the abstract goal of compensation, it appears not to typically result in support for concrete action to help suffering outgroups. Anger however, *does* tend to motivate concrete actions.

On this view, guilt appears more likely to engender certain responses, such as apologies and compensation, than those we might view as constituting compassionate helping. Indeed, Faulkner (2014b) summarises research evidence to suggest that guilt is extremely limited in regard to compassionate action (see, e.g., Lickel et al. 2011; Iyer and Leach 2010; Harth et al. 2008). In contrast, anger – particularly when it is framed as empathic and/or is provoked by moral outrage – seems to bear some form of causal relationship to compassionate helping by directing is in particular ways, that is, in terms of both tackling the causes of suffering and seeking to address and alleviate suffering (see, e.g., van Zomeren et al. 2004; Iyer et al. 2007; Iyer and Leach 2010). Hoffman (2000, pp. 100–101; emphasis added) illustrates the connection between anger and compassion by citing a letter to the *New York Times* written in the mid-1980s in which the author asserted that 'the pictures of starving children in Ethiopia are heart-wrenching, but feeling sad isn't enough...we send a check, the pictures disappear from TV screens, and soon we forget that millions are dying...Instead we should feel *outraged* that in a world of plenty hunger still exists. *Outrage* produces action'.

If we accept that anger can, and does, stimulate compassion two further questions immediately arise. The first is whether anger may, by its very nature, be of concern – resulting in excessive actions and, perhaps, violence in the name of compassion. Clearly of importance here is a form of anger, mediated and framed through a discernment of its appropriate extent and ends. Whitebrook (2014, p. 25), for example, presents 'compassionate anger' as a form of 'defensible anger' mediated by rational deliberation through which those witnessing suffering 'make judgements as to its cause and decisions about appropriate action'. While not wishing to suggest that all compassionate anger is appropriately directed and enacted, what can serve to prevent anger from going too far is precisely compassion's concern for one's fellow human. In this way, other components of compassion – such as empathy – can humanise anger and, in turn, practical wisdom works to ensure that that anger is focused in a way that leads to an appropriate enactment of compassion. As Whitebrook (2014, p. 30) suggests,

> Compassionate political anger will not generally lead to violence, and the risk that it might is not itself sufficient to disbar it from politics altogether: that risk should not place a limitation *per se* on recognising the viability of a working idea of compassion in which anger plays a part.

Appropriately framed and enacted compassionate anger, then, is an anger in concord with reason, avoiding an excess of rashness. For this reason, there is no need to remove anger from compassion completely – only for it to be moderated effectively by our compassionate deliberations (see also, Nussbaum 2001).

The second question raised by an acceptance of anger as an emotion which can support the motivation of compassionate action is whether it can act in such a motivating way alone. That is, whether anger can be involved without some other emotion – in particular, pity, sympathy or empathy. For Faulkner (2014b) anger *can* act alone in inducing compassionate helping, but this seems to me to go too far. Certainly, it would seem likely (and as we have seen there is social psychological evidence to suggest that this is the case) that anger can stimulate compassionate helping but to suggest that it can do so in isolation from other emotions such as those focused on within this chapter seems overly reductionist (if not psychologically impossible). It would seem likely, that is, that where anger is involved, this is likely to be *in relation to and as building on* the other forms of emotional responses examined here.

Conclusion

This chapter has examined those emotions – pity, sympathy, empathy and, to a lesser extent, anger – central to compassion. Understanding these emotions is of paramount importance for conceiving compassion, given that compassion is a virtue which stems from an emotional response. Understood as involving both affective and cognitive capacities, and against a background of contested understandings, I have suggested that particular understandings of pity, sympathy, empathy and anger are necessary for compassion. Furthermore, I have argued that these emotions stand in relation to others aspects of compassion – notably care for others and what might broadly be understood as helping behaviour. As such, the emotions, in concord with reason, play a crucial role in motivating and shaping compassionate acts. In the next chapter our focus shifts to compassionate acts, including how these can be conceived, what forms they can take, and at what target they can aim.

Notes

1. It should be noted that Snow also includes grief in this family of emotions.
2. https://www.youtube.com/watch?v=1Evwgu369Jw
3. See, for example, Nietzche (1881/1997) and Arendt (1963) for leading criticisms of compassion.
4. It should be noted here that for Rousseau, so far as *pitié* is concerned, we may act in an 'unreflecting' manner.

5. Readers should note, again, that translations of Rousseau use the term 'pity' to refer to what here I am referring to as sympathy as it relates to compassion.

6. While I seek to separate them, both of these readings can be seen in Adam Smith's (1759/2009, pp. 15; 13–14) suggestions that 'grief and joy ... strongly expressed in the look and gestures of any one, at once affect the spectator with some degree of a like painful or agreeable emotion' and that 'by the imagination we place ourselves in the other's situation, we conceive ourselves enduring all the same torments, we enter as it were into his body, and become in some measure the same person with him, and thence form some idea of his sensations, and even feel something which, though weaker in degree, is not altogether unlike them'.

7. In their analysis Wilhelm and Bekkers (2010, p. 12) explain, for example, that 'a large portion of this evidence is from experiments that manipulate empathy in specific situations'. In their review of empirical evidence on empathy published in the mid-1980s, Eisenberg and Miller (1987, p. 114) point out that empirical studies have tended to focus on empathy for the object of participant's helping behaviour in a specific situation, which would tend to be more likely than one's helping is for others beyond the object/situation.

8. 'Often, empathetic reconstruction will involve compassion, but empathy is not necessary for compassion as I understand it, since compassion can, as in the case of neonates, take the primitive form of mere pain or distress in the presence of the pain or distress of others, independently of any imaginative reconstruction' (Crisp 2008, p. 234).

9. It is because of this imaginative gap that Nussbaum (2001, p. 328) places great importance on the role of literature in educating for empathy on the basis that 'only in fiction is the mind of the other transparent. The empathetic person attempts to reconstruct the mental experience of another'. This point is returned to in Chap. 6.

CHAPTER 4

Compassionate Acts

INTRODUCTION

Over the first three chapters compassion has been characterised as a virtue drawing out of our emotions; a virtue, that is, the meaning and enactment of which stems from a given feeling. In the case of compassion, this feeling is in the form of a sorrow occasioned by the suffering of others, deepened by empathy, and given further meaning by a sense of care or fellow-feeling for those who are suffering. As a virtue, we can understand compassion as a morally positive character trait or disposition which is, at least in part, formed and expressed in action. Indeed, if compassion is to be more than reducible to a particular morally relevant emotional state, albeit one which involves reason, how we *enact* compassion seems crucial.

Across the literature on compassion various terms are used for active responses which seek to alleviate the suffering of others. We saw in the last chapter that psychological literature conceives such actions as 'helping behaviour' (see, e.g., Eisenberg and Miller 1987), while philosophical literature has tended to use the terms 'beneficent action' (Nussbaum 2001) or 'beneficent actions' (Blum 1987). In this chapter, I will use the term 'compassionate acts'. My reason for doing so is the belief that while all compassionate actions are in some form beneficent, not all beneficent actions necessarily stem from compassion. Compassionate actions are, therefore, actions which are beneficent but which stem from a response to the suffering of others, involve empathic distress, and are mediated by the principle of care, rather than from some other cognitive or affective disposition, such as gratitude or kindness.

© The Author(s) 2017
A. Peterson, *Compassion and Education*,
DOI 10.1057/978-1-137-54838-2_4

Within the previous chapters compassionate acts have been conceived in broad terms, with the following suggestions relevant to compassionate acts being made. First, that emotions, and in particular pity, sympathy and empathic distress, play a crucial role in motivating compassionate acts. Second, that while empathic distress and the principle of care motivate compassionate action, the latter has a stronger association and, as such, plays an important role in mediating action – particularly those which are planned and long-term. Third, that the deliberation central to practical wisdom plays a crucial role in assessing the available alternatives and determining the right action, at the right time, for the right people, for the right reason, in the right way. Fourth, that deliberating about and assessing available alternatives takes account of salient person and contextually specific characteristics relevant to the given situation. Through these various processes the compassionate subject moves 'from a state of being a receiver of information, that is too say, of being a spectator, observer or listener, into that of being an actor' (Boltanski 1999, p. 31).

CONCEIVING COMPASSIONATE ACTION – SOME CRITICAL QUESTIONS

From the outset it is important to ascertain the scope of compassionate action. To commence this task, two initial comments are necessary. First, and perhaps most obviously, compassion *motivates* our action with respect to the suffering of others. While such actions in this regard (which are the main focus of this chapter) are aimed predominantly at *alleviating* suffering, we should be mindful that there will also be occasions when alleviation is not possible and is, therefore not the aim. In such situations, supporting those suffering to *endure* their pain while maintaining their dignity becomes the aim. Second, while compassion motivates actions, it also *frames* our responses in particular situations. This is most clearly seen in judicial cases, where juries return verdicts which are just when framed in terms of compassion rather than accordance with the law. In England in the 1990s, for example, a number of courts heard cases of individuals charged with growing cannabis – a criminal offence – for the use of themselves or those close to them in order to alleviate the pain of chronic conditions, such as multiple sclerosis or spinal pain (Marks 1998; BBC 1999). Contradicting the law, juries in these cases returned verdicts which were framed by a compassionate response to the suffering based on the recognition that the motivation of those charged was not self-interest or criminal intent, but alleviating suffering. In these cases, compassion mediated how justice was conceived and enacted (Solokon 2006), reminding us of the interconnection between the virtues.

In addition to these basic remarks, it is important to make a further fundamental – though again perhaps somewhat obvious – point. This is that, frequently, when moved by the suffering of others, the range of actions available to compassionate agents are likely to be wide and various. That this is so is exemplified by responses to the European Migrant Crisis. Governments, media outlets, humanitarian organisations, and religious groups alike made clear the form that possible responses from compassionate citizens[1] could be (see, e.g., Home Office and Department for Communities and Local Government 2015; Richards 2015; Weaver 2015). The possibilities offered included giving money, donating other items, protesting, volunteering with grass-roots, national or international groups, signing a petition, direct action, and providing housing for those seeking asylum.

Given the range of options available in many situations where others are suffering, how can we make sense of choosing which compassionate action is the most appropriate one? To some extent, the answer lies back in the analysis of Chap. 2. Here, the role of practical wisdom in deliberating about and discerning the right action was viewed as central to conceiving compassion as a virtue. The deliberating agent takes into account a range of agent- and context-specific factors in order to discern what the right action might be. To this end, it is useful to posit a number of questions of compassionate action which can shed light on the sorts of considerations which are likely to be involved.

The first question we can ask in respect of compassionate action is whether such action *is focused on spontaneous, short-term* or *planned, long-term behaviour*. It was considered in the last section that this distinction is crucial within psychological studies of empathy and compassion, which typically draw on experimental conditions associated with spontaneous helping. Within religious traditions, and here the Christian parable of the Good Samaritan provides an illustration, compassionate acts primarily focus on spontaneous, short-term actions, with the subject of compassion in close proximity to the compassionate object (in the parable, the Samaritan). Of course, a compassionate act which starts as spontaneous and short-term can grow into something planned and longer. In the introduction to this book, the example was given of local beautician Katie Cutler's response to the physical assault of Alan Barnes, a 67-year-old man with disabilities living in the North East of England. Her response – to launch a twitter appeal in the hope of raising a small amount of funds (£500) – grew into a larger, longer-term activity requiring much greater thought and planning than was the case with her immediate, spontaneous response, including establishing a foundation to help others.

These reflections in respect of spontaneous, short-term and planned, long-term compassionate acts highlight a number of further questions which help to get to the heart of compassionate action. These include the following:

1. *whether the compassionate act is enacted in respect of an individual* (the traveller in the case of the Good Samaritan; Alan Barnes in the case of Katie Cutler) *or a more general group or collectivity* (when we donate money to a help communities affected by a natural disaster, for example). Here, what commences as a compassionate act in respect of an individual may grow into acts in respect of a larger group. Similarly, compassionate acts in respect of a larger group may become more focused on the situations of individuals;

2. *whether the compassionate act is enacted individually* (again, as was the case with the Good Samaritan) *or collectively* (when we become a member of a charitable organisation, for example). Here, the possibility of individual actions transforming into collective actions must be recognised;

3. *whether the compassionate act is enacted in respect of a known other or an unknown other.* Here, and again as the case of Katie Cutler and Alan Barnes illustrates, compassionate acts can move object and subject from strangers to some form of relationship in which they come to know each other.

An additional question we may ask is *whether the compassionate action is shaped by the object or the subject, or indeed through some sort of exchange between the two.* This question seems particularly relevant given the suggestion made in previous chapters that, at least in the first instance and until some form of dialogue has occurred, compassion depends on the understanding of suffering and the sufferer held by the compassionate subject. Given this, and owing to a range of possible factors, compassionate acts might be well intentioned but may miss the mark from the position of the object. The example was given in Chap. 2 of international aid responses to the earthquake in Nepal in 2015. In this example, while the sending of food products to help those in need appeared an appropriate compassionate act, the sending of tuna fish and mayonnaise seemed to misjudge the intentions and actual needs of those suffering.

It is important, then, that we ask in respect of compassionate acts how such acts are understood and determined by the compassionate objects *and* subjects involved.[2] This involves raising some difficult and complex subjects. What if the traveller on the road to Jericho had not wanted to be helped by a Samaritan and, on realising that he had been helped by the Samaritan, had failed to reciprocate the Samaritan's openness to his fellow man? Is it compassionate for a soldier to save the life of a dying enemy from an opposing force out of a concern for his humanity, when that solider would rather die with his comrades? What represents a compassionate act when a person is dying from a loss of blood but does not wish to receive a blood transfusion because of their religious commitment? Does our response to this last question change when the person is a baby, and the religious views are those of her parents who are deciding on her behalf?

An additional example illustrates the tentative point I am seeking to make in this regard about the morally salient relevance of the object's outlook. Let us say that Steven has a colleague who is suffering as a result of a painful medical condition. Steven is aware that both he and his colleague, Sarah, are active participants in a particular faith community and that, owing to their faith, praying together represents – for them – a compassionate, helping action in response to the suffering. On this account, while we may or may not share their faith, there seem to be no prima facie reasons for rejecting prayer as a compassionate act. Now let's consider a similar situation, but one in which Sarah is an active participant in a faith community, whilst Steven is agnostic. In this situation we might still say that prayer is a compassionate act, though this time things do not seem so clear cut. One would want to know more about how both Sarah and Steven think and feel about prayer before making a reasoned judgement. Similarly, let us now consider a situation in which Steven has a strong faith and in which Sarah is an atheist. In fact, Sarah dismisses the validity of religious beliefs completely. I think we would like to say that in such a situation Sarah's views *are* an important moral feature, and that as such Steven should take them into account in his reasoning (i.e. whether praying together is an appropriate, compassionate response). Whilst this does not mean that the sufferer's views necessarily trump those of others involved in the situation, it does mean that these views are far from irrelevant and, indeed, that they are important moral considerations which need to be accounted for in any analysis of compassion.

To summarise, this section, the questions raised here can help us to analyse some key features and dimensions of compassionate action. The answers to each of the questions identified here may not, of course, always be straightforward, and are likely to be fluid over time. Such fluidity will also be brought about on occasions where the morally salient features of a situation change. To give a brief example to illustrate this point, we can imagine, for example, the flow of compassion and compassionate acts for a person whose house has been burgled being fundamentally disrupted if evidence came to light that the person was a burglar themselves. Here, sentiments and reasons change as more information comes to light.

Compassionate Acts – Transforming the Road to Jericho?

In his first public anti-war speech, delivered in the context of the Vietnam War, Martin Luther King Jr (1967) argued that

> A true revolution of values will soon cause us to question the fairness and justice of many of our past and present policies. On the one hand we are called to play the Good Samaritan on life's roadside, but that will be only an initial act. One day we must come to see that the whole Jericho road must be transformed so that men and women will not be constantly beaten and robbed as they make their journey on life's highway. True compassion is more than flinging a coin to a beggar. It comes to see than an edifice which produces beggars needs restructuring.

In these words, Martin Luther King evocatively delineates a central concern for many advocates of compassion; namely, the desire to take compassionate acts beyond the immediate help and care for those suffering in ways which address the structural origins of their suffering. The worry associated with a focus on help is two-fold. First, that helping forms of compassionate actions are primarily short-term, palliative measures which fail to challenge and address the actual causes of suffering. Second, that help can be conceived – and here again the importance of the compassionate object's intentions raised in the last section resurfaces – as patronising, ignoring the agency of those suffering and representing them as 'helpless'. Indicative of this premise is the quotation referenced in Chap. 2 and often attributed to Aboriginal elder, activist and educator Lilla Watson: 'If you have come here to help me, you are wasting your time. But if you have come because your liberation is bound up with mine, then let us work together'.

The concern to differentiate between helping and challenging structural factors can be identified in recent writings on compassion, within which there has been a desire to distinguish between compassionate acts which focus on *caring* and those which focus on *justice*. Ure and Frost (2014) offer a useful exposition of the parable of the Good Samaritan in order to illustrate the differences which are posited in such accounts. After recounting the key details of the parable, they suggest that

> the Good Samaritan pays no heed to the legal, criminal or political context of the event. The Samaritan responds exclusively to the fact of the victim's suffering. The Samaritan's compassionate response begins with his dressing of the victim's wound and ends with his payment to a third party to nurse the man back to health...At no point, however, does the parable indicate that the Samaritan's compassion might entail that he address the victim's legal or political circumstances. The Samaritan remedies the immediate harm inflicted on the victim, but he shows no concern about the causes of his suffering or interest in remedying these causes. (Ure and Frost 2014, p. 6)

In their work on compassion in education, Arnot et al. (2009) distinguish between *compassion as caring* and *compassion as justice* (a little later in this section I will raise a significant issue for those who wish to appeal to notions of justice in relation to compassion from a broadly cosmopolitan/human rights position). While 'compassion as caring' is based on concern for those who are suffering, 'compassion as justice' focuses on the provision of more focused and sustained support for those who suffer, including challenging and seeking to redress the causes of the sufferers' plight. Exploring teacher perceptions of working with asylum seeking and refugee children, they suggest that

> A particular conceptual distinction was especially helpful differentiating between: first a concept of compassion based on the need to *care* for and help those who have suffered in their lives and seek help and shelter – this notion is based on *concern (whether empathy, sympathy or pity)* for those who are victims of circumstances; and secondly, a concept of compassion in terms of *justice* – offering help for those who are in trouble on the basis of notions of *equality and human rights*. (2009, pp. 252–253)

For Arnot, et al. the value of understanding compassion as justice lies (1) in its emphasis on human rights and (2) in its focus on seeking to challenge and address societal issues that cause, or at least render possible, the suffering in question. Identifying certain traditions[3] as committed to notions of caring, they argue that

> One major limitation of these traditions... is that they do not consider the ways in which compassion might transcend from the individual to society or address the causes of such vulnerability or distress – the social and moral responsibility for the suffering of the other.

We need to be careful, though, about how we employ this distinction between compassion as caring and compassion as justice. While the care/justice distinction is of some value in considering the intended telos of compassionate acts, there are reasons why drawing overly sharp distinctions is less helpful.

On a fairly rudimentary level, the distinction appears to be more useful in the abstract than it is in reality. For example, when Ebony is exposed to the suffering of Edward, and in doing so feels compassion for Edward, a number of actions may be possible for Ebony. These may take the form of expressing concern and caring for Edward on an intimate and personal level, or they may take the form of working to address the particular wider socio-political issues that could be said to have caused or heightened the suffering. The path that Ebony takes will depend on the particular contextual features of the suffering experienced by Edward and the exposure of Ebony to this. Such contextual features are likely to include the relationship between Ebony and Edward, the proximity of Ebony to Edward, the wider networks of support available to both, and the actual abilities and efficacy Ebony possesses in relation to supporting Edward, as well as a wide range of other more practical concerns. Crucially, through deliberation and discernment, Ebony aims at the right form of action – caring, justice or both – after assessing the non-morally and morally salient features of the situation. In some situations, caring, rather than justice, may simply be the appropriate compassionate response.

One reason, then, for wishing to hold on to the idea that compassionate actions can justifiably take the form of caring responses is that there may well be cases in which practical wisdom determines a caring, rather than justice, response as the right form of action to take. In addition, there is a second reason for maintaining compassion as caring – one which was introduced in the last section. This is the idea that rather than being distinct, caring and justice are intimately intertwined. Indeed, there are certain compelling reasons why the relationship between the two should be viewed as symbiotic. Not least, and as discussed in the last chapter, the principle of care is a crucial feature associated with compassionate action, particularly where planned, long-term actions are concerned. Moreover, when we look closely at actual examples of compassionate action both caring and justice often seem to be involved. We can see this relationship in the following two examples of compassionate actions – one spontaneous and one planned.

In 1937, Mario Tonelli played as a fullback for the University of Notre Dame. In a game against the University of Southern Carolina, with the teams tied at 6–6, Tonelli made a game changing 70-yard run late in the fourth quarter. He scored the winning touchdown shortly after. In 1942 Tonelli found himself in a vastly different setting – the Bataan Peninsula on the Philippine Islands. As an American serviceman, Tonelli was one of the thousands of prisoners-of-war forced to take part in what has become known as the Bataan Death March. The March was brutal, with many prisoners beaten, bayoneted and killed. Many also died through starvation, exhaustion or disease. One day on the march, Tonelli was approached by a guard who had been taking possessions from the prisoners. He was ordered to hand over a gold ring. Under provocation and threat of death, Tonelli handed over the ring – his Notre Dame class ring. Moments later an officer approached Tonelli, asking whether one of his men had taken something from him. Tonelli explained that his ring had been taken. The officer held out the ring to Tonelli, ordering him to hide it from sight so that it would not be taken again. Why had the officer returned the ring? As he explained to Tonelli, 'I was educated in America...At the University of Southern California. I know a little about the famous Notre Dame football team. In fact, I watched you beat USC in 1937. I know how much this ring means to you, so I wanted to get it back to you[4].' Here, a shared moment in the past had revisited the humanity between the two actors. In extreme circumstances, amidst acute injustices and a lack of humanity, came a fleeting spark of humanity in which both care and justice seem – just for a brief moment in time – to be involved.

In 2015, British teacher and French resident, Mary Jones established a library at the migrant camp (known commonly as 'The Jungle') in Calais, France. Named the Jungle Books Library (or *Livres de la Jungle*), the Library was an extension of Jones' long-standing donation of books to those residing in the camp. As the library has developed, its support has expanded to incorporate technologies, language learning classes, as well as a Jungle Books Kids Restaurant to provide meals for unaccompanied children. Fundamentally, the Jungle Library provides a place and space for people to engage with each other on a human level. Explaining her decision to establish the library, Jones suggests that she 'wanted to start something that offered real, practical help' because 'many people here are well-educated – they want to get on and they want books that will help them read and write English, apply for jobs, fill-in forms' (cited in Bausells 2015). Again, here is a compassionate act which involves caring for others and their humanity while also seeking to respond to issues of justice through establishing mechanisms of support beyond the immediate present. The intention is to reach a position in which migrants will run the library themselves (Tagholm 2015).

Before concluding this section, there is another reason for seeking clarity about what compassion as justice precisely means, one which is often hinted at within educational literature on compassion but which generally remains somewhat vague. This need for clarity concerns whether compassion as justice is derived from forms of cosmopolitanism based on Kantian notions of duties/responsibilities. In resting the importance of compassion as justice on human rights, positions such as that taken by Arnot et al. present compassion as justice in largely duty-based terms. This carries with it, however, certain important implications which become clearer through a brief examination of scholarship on cosmopolitan approaches to global justice.

Though they do not always employ the terms 'compassion' or 'caring', cosmopolitan theorists interested in global justice and the need to 'do justice' (Jones 2002) frequently identify a significant shift from forms of *beneficence* which might be seen as morally praiseworthy (such as certain forms of charitable altruism) to other forms of response to doing justice based on *duties* to others. This ethic of mutual obligation includes two distinct, though related, duties acting on humans. The first – a negative duty which we might call the 'no-harm principle' – entails that citizens be 'aware of, and accountable for, the consequences of actions, direct or indirect, intended or unintended, which may radically restrict or delimit the choices or others' (Held 2010, pp. 70–71). The second, of particular relevance to our discussion of compassion, is a positive duty which we might call the 'justice principle'. This is the principle that one should act when the humanity and dignity of others is threatened, even if this threat is not of one's own making and wherever in the world others may live. How we understand and interpret the 'justice principle' clearly matters a great deal. The distinction Linklater (1998, p. 206) makes between thin and thick conceptions of cosmopolitan citizenship is relevant here: 'thin conceptions of cosmopolitan citizenship revolve around compassion for the vulnerable but leave asymmetries of power and wealth intact; thick conceptions of cosmopolitan citizenship attempt to influence the structural conditions faced by vulnerable groups'. So far so reasonably straightforward. The thick conceptions of cosmopolitanism identified by Linklater appear very close – if not identical – to compassion as justice.

However, proponents of thick cosmopolitanism frequently go one step further in their understanding of obligations. That is, they locate political and ethical obligations to challenge and address injustice (or to enact compassion as justice) in notions of 'complicity' (Andreotti 2006) or 'causal responsibility' (Dobson 2006). On these accounts, complicity or causal responsibility result from a range of factors, including the historical and contemporary implications of colonialism and the unequal impact of economic globalisation (Parekh 2003). The work of Thomas Pogge (2002, 2005), for instance, has been central in asserting the complicity, and resulting responsibility, of those in the Global North to the injustices faced by the Global South. According to Pogge (2005, p. 33),

> by shaping and enforcing the social conditions that foreseeably and avoidably cause the monumental suffering of global poverty, we are harming the global poor – or, to put it more descriptively, we are active participants in the largest, though not the gravest, crime against humanity ever committed.

The overtly strong form of cosmopolitanism advocated by Pogge may not be for the fainthearted, given that it entails that for people living in Westernised nations even to be passive is to do harm to others and, as such, is to be complicit in perpetrating and maintaining global social injustices. In this vain, Pogge (2005, p. 37) adds:

> today's massive and severe poverty manifests a violation by the affluent of their negative duties: an immense crime in which we affluent citizens of the rich countries (as well as the political and economic 'elites' of most poor countries) are implicated.

Positions such as that taken by Pogge provide a particular way of conceiving justice at a global level – one in which simply enjoying the inequitable benefits of globalisation is sufficient for placing significant moral duties on both action and the form that such action takes. One would assume that, on such accounts, some of the forms of action we might equate with compassion as caring (donating food to survivors of a natural disaster, for example) would be viewed as further instantiations of economic, cultural and political hegemony and dominance (i.e. the Global North as saviour, the Global South as in need of saviour), carrying with them the possibility of 'collapsing' into what Hickling-Hudson (2011, p. 461) terms 'palliative charity'. Such positioning differs from less stringent accounts of the relationship between morally equal human beings which are more likely to understand caring actions as 'stating an important duty, and as [requiring] quite as much action – if not more – than appeals to justice' (Dower 1991, p. 274).

Recognition of complicity is also claimed to play a crucial motivational role. Linklater (2006, p. 3), the 'cosmopolitan emotions' necessary to engender action are 'most likely to develop when actors believe they are causally responsible for harming others and their physical environment'. Similarly, for Dobson (2006, p. 172) 'if I cause someone harm I am required as a matter of justice to rectify that harm. If, on the other hand, I bear no responsibility for the harm, justice requires nothing of me – and although beneficence might be desirable I cannot be held to account... for not exercising it'. Yet, such statements appear troubling for conceiving compassion as justice, if we understand justice through an ethical cosmopolitan framework. What appears to be important in motivating compassionate acts to address structural causes of suffering on this account is precisely the compassionate agents' culpability – however diffused and indirect – for bringing the suffering about in the first place. Yet, it is far from clear – and there is currently little written about – whether we can truly be compassionate for suffering for which we, ourselves are culpable in causing. While I do not intend to examine this point in detail here, it does seem to me reasonable to suggest that those wishing to draw stronger distinctions between compassion and caring need to say something more about notions of culpability in relation to compassion.

In this section, I have argued that both caring and justice are useful in conceiving and examining the intentions and aims of compassionate act. I have also sought to suggest that while this distinction serves certain purposes, drawing it too sharply runs the risk of separating caring from justice in ways that are unhelpful. In any given situation, the sorts of deliberation and discernment central to practical wisdom play a role in forming a judgements about action, which include weighing and weighting concerns of caring and justice relevant to the specific situation. So far in this chapter, then, what form compassionate action takes and the considerations involved have been explored. In the next section, the focus shifts somewhat to consider real and potential barriers to compassionate action.

BARRIERS TO COMPASSIONATE ACTION

The purpose of this section is to examine pertinent and relevant factors which can act as barriers to compassionate action. In taking this focus, it is necessary to frame the discussion which follows. Clearly, there a range of factors could readily identify as prohibiting compassionate acts. These could reasonably be said to include a range of personal characteristics/ vices, such narcissism, selfishness, envy, greed, ignorance and callousness, as well as more practical constraints, such as time, money, physical location, available information and existing commitments. My intention is not to focus on *all* such factors (to do so would clearly be beyond the confines of this book). Instead, in being interested in potential constraints on compassionate action, attention will be on those factors which we can understand as directly prohibiting compassion where one might reasonably expect compassionate actions to occur. Surveying the literature on compassion, three particular barriers to compassionate action are frequently cited: the diffusion of responsibility/bystander affect, situational constraints and helplessness/compassion fatigue. These are now considered in turn.

Why Me? The Diffusion of Responsibility and the Bystander Effect

An important barrier to compassion is the extent to which those in a position to help may simply ask: 'why me?' (Miller 2002). This concern has a number of important facets. On one level, the answer to this concern is provided by the very definition of compassion. On this reading, the answer to 'why me?' is 'because I am a particular type of person, one who cares for others, recognises common humanity and shared fragility, exhibits empathic distress, and makes some form of *eudaimonistic* judgement about the suffering of others'. However, the challenge of 'why me?' runs deeper, particularly when it is framed in terms of 'why me, rather than other people who are also placed – maybe even better placed – to help than me?'. Miller (2002) categorises possible reasons why one may fail to act in this regard as owing to (1) people interpreting the inaction of others as a sign of the lack of urgency and/or need; (2) people responding to and replicating the norms of the group (in this case inaction, though studies suggest that the opposite is also true – that action can induce action from others); and, (3) to the diffusion of responsibility. This diffusion of responsibility can be conceived in situations where the potential helpers are *numerous* (e.g. why should it be me who should help those suffering from famine elsewhere in the world when there are many others who are equally, or perhaps even better, placed to help?) and in situations where the potential helpers are *fewer* (e.g. why should it be me who should help this person who has fallen over and is injured, when there are several other people around who are equally, or perhaps even better, placed to help?).

On a larger scale, a good deal of attention has been paid to notions of responsibility, and its diffusion, in literature involving global ethics (see notably, Singer 1993; Unger 1996; Appiah 2007). Within this largely theoretical work the notion of doing one's *fair share* has become prominent as a particular, cosmopolitan response. In such accounts, individuals are expected to undertake only what might reasonably be seen to comprise their own fair share – though what amounts to one's fair share is often dependent on particular agent-centred calculations (see, e.g., Murphy 2000; Appiah 2007). This places particular strains on the compassionate agent, who must include in their deliberations what one's fair share actually is. Thus, and as Miller (2002, p. 119) remarks, while 'altruism is an extremely important contributor to the quality of our lives, whether one is thinking of urgent life-threatening situations, or simply of everyday acts of helplessness, giving directions, picking up the spilled shopping and so on, and we ought all to do our bit... none of us can tell what that bit amounts to'.

If we turn to empirical work on actor motivations, research presents a varied picture concerning the role of character and dispositions (such as compassion) in motivating action. It is both interesting and important to note that while notions of compassion, altruism, common humanity and solidarity often appear in the *rhetoric* of factors motivating humanitarianism and volunteering in support of others who are suffering (see, for example,

Baughan and Fiori 2015; UNGA 2016), empirical evidence on the factors which motivate and sustain helping actions presents a complex picture and is not particularly instructive so far as the diffusion of responsibility is concerned. This said, empirical evidence on the motivations of philanthropists (understood widely as those donating money to charitable causes) and volunteers[5] does highlight several points of relevance for our understanding of compassionate action which it is worth elucidating briefly here. First and foremost, in reports of such motivations values such as compassion provide only one element in the myriad of complex factors which motivate volunteers. A range of studies support the existence of multiple motivations, though different studies configure these slightly differently. In a meta-review of studies of philanthropy, Bekkers and Wiepking (2011) posit eight categories: awareness of need, being asked, the costs and benefits of giving, altruism, personal reputation, psychological benefits, and personal values and efficacy (see also Rochester 2006; Body and Breeze 2016). In addition, such studies suggest that altruistic and value-based motivations such as compassion are rarely the most important in understanding action. At best, they sit alongside motivations we can consider as self-interested – such as developing new skills, enhancing employability or meeting new people (Stebbins 2004; Rochester 2006; Rochester et al. 2009).[6] In a study examining motivations for volunteering among higher education students, Holdsworth (2010) reports that positive impacts on others were viewed primarily as an outcome rather than a motivation for action. Interview data in the study did 'not reveal a group of students motivated by personal values, but rather a group of students willing to test themselves and try out new experiences and meet new people with the expectation of being able to make some form of contribution' (2010, p. 431). For this group of respondents, only when religious commitments were involved did the notion of a good person doing good become pronounced. Furthermore, there are a range of socio-economic and cultural factors, some of them fairly straightforward, which aid or limit people's action. As Rochester (2006, p. 13) reflects, 'the great majority of people who volunteer do so' simply 'because they have been asked'.

Second, empirical evidence suggests that where personal characteristics and values are involved, these are directed in particular – and sometimes highly uneven – ways across different actions, causes and groups. Evidence suggests that support for different causes varies for a number of reasons. Some causes (often those related to certain medical conditions) are more popular than others. Studies of causes receiving the most charitable financial support in the UK, for example, suggest that such giving 'varies widely between both causes and individual charities' (Body and Breeze 2016, p. 58). Evidence also suggests that helping in relation to particular causes is often spurred by some form of personal connection (Payton and Moody 2008) and is more likely when actors see some similarity between themselves and those they are seeking to help (Sanghera 2016). In addition, data from the USA suggests that personal values and characteristics are more important in determining financial donations to causes than they are for giving time. So far as giving time is concerned existing connections and ties appear more central (Jones 2006; see also Rochester 2006).

Third, data on motivations for planned, long-term actions typically involves self-report mechanisms which, as such, may well overplay the importance of values (Rochester 2006). It is notable that motivations related to compassion, those for example which include altruism based on a recognition of common humanity and solidarity with sufferers, are usually strongest and clearest when we consider the individual biographies and stories of actors involved. This point regarding self-reporting becomes increasingly important when we flip our focus to reasons why people *do not* take action (which, returning to the principle of diffusion is a central concern). Empirical research typically reports that barriers are largely structural and/or practical and include socio-economic status, time, knowledge of opportunity, and work and familial commitments. Few, if any, are likely to report that they do not act because of a lack of compassion, care or concern for others!

To summarise, empirical research provides little clarity as far as the dispersion of responsibility in relation to planned actions such as philanthropy and volunteering are concerned. While it would seem that personal characteristics and values *do* play some role in motivating actions associated with philanthropy and volunteering, this role is not only nuanced but has to be understood in relation to a range of other factors – including those of self-interest (to which we return in the next chapter). Personal characteristics and values, such as compassion, it seems can only tell us part of the story in understanding such action. Yet they remain part of the story nevertheless.

What role, though, does the dispersion of responsibility associated with the presence of others play at more localised and proximal levels? A number of studies of helping behaviour interested in what is known commonly as the *bystander effect* have shown that the amount of people present and witnessing suffering affects how likely it is that people will help. A range of psychological studies (see, e.g., Darley and Latané 1968; Latané and Dabbs 1975; Latané and Nida 1981) provide evidence which indicates that the higher the number of *potential* helpers, the less likely it is that individuals will take responsibility to act. In their seminal study, Darley and Latané (1968) detail various features of the bystander effect. The study itself was inspired by the real life case of Kitty Genovese, a young woman stabbed to death in the early hours when returning to her apartment block. The *New York Times* (Gansberg 1964) reported that:

> For more than half and hour 38 respectable, law-abiding citizens in Queens watched a killer stalk and stab a women in three separate attacks in Kew Gardens. Twice the sound of their voices and the sudden glow of their bedroom lights interrupted him and frightened him off. Each time he returned, sought her out and stabbed her again. Not one person telephoned the police during the assault; one witness called after the woman was dead.

Though they had the opportunity to help themselves, or to call for help from others, good people had done nothing. This was despite hearing the victim scream 'Oh, my God, he stabbed me! Please help me! Please help me!', and then later, 'I'm dying, I'm dying, I'm dying'. The police made clear afterwards that if they had been called at the time of the first attack, Kitty Genovese would probably have lived. When asked why they had not helped responses varied, and included misunderstanding the seriousness of the situation, not wanting to get involved, and tiredness, while some said that they just did not know why they had not helped.

In their study on bystander intervention, Darley and Latané (1968) describe the diffusion of responsibility behind the bystander effect in the following terms:

> When only one bystander is present in an emergency, if help is to come, it must come from him. Although he may choose to ignore it ... any pressure to intervene focuses uniquely on him. When there are several observers present, however, the pressures to intervene do not focus on any one of the observers; instead the responsibility for intervention is shared among all onlookers and is not unique to any one. As a result, no one helps.

This supposition is suggested too by their findings. Undertaking a discussion about college life through an intercom system, participants faced with an interlocutor suffering from a seizure, were less likely to call for help when there were others involved than if they thought they were the only one able to help.[7] The study revealed that whereas 85 % of participants reported the seizure when they thought they were the only one who knew, this figure fell to 31 % of participants when they thought that four others were present. In addition, Darley and Latané (1968, p. 380) reported that 'every one of the subjects in the two-person groups, but only sixty-two per cent of the subjects in the six-person groups ever reported the emergency'. Other, more recent studies seem to confirm the bystander effect, including the ways in which the age, gender, the clothing of the sufferer and the reactions of different potential respondents affect action/in-action.[8]

Interestingly, given the principle of diffusion of responsibility, Darley and Latané present a more complex picture regarding why participants did not respond. For these participants, there was not a conscious decision *not* to respond. Instead, Darley and Latané (1968, p. 382) present a picture of 'indecision and conflict concerning whether to respond or not'. In other words, non-action was not the result of character, but rather the result of other, situational, factors. They conclude 'the explanation of bystander "apathy" may lie more in the bystander's response to other observers than in presumed personality deficiencies of "apathetic" individuals'.

It has been suggested here that notions of the diffusion of responsibility and the bystander effect can play a role in the framing of compassionate action. To reiterate a general point first, support for these principles can be found in theoretical literature for situations in which potential helpers are both numerous and fewer, and in empirical literature for situations in which potential helpers are fewer (empirical literature for situations in which potential helpers are numerous are largely silent about the diffusion of responsibility).

More specifically, I would like to make the following tentative points, regarding what the principles of the diffusion of responsibility and the bystander effect suggest in relation to compassion. First, clearly, when the situation is immediate and requires spontaneous compassionate action, there may be situational factors at play – meaning that personality and character are not the total explanation for action/non-action (a point to which we return below). However, while this seems broadly acceptable on a prima facie basis for immediate, spontaneous cases, it is not certain that such explanations are quite so apposite when we move to other situations in which there is more time to deliberate and discern the appropriate course of action. What is so puzzling about the inaction in the case of Kitty Genovese is precisely that the decisions not to act were made over a longer time period, as not once but three times her killer returned. The second point, which builds on this reflection, is to reiterate that when we consider the motivations and decisions regarding compassionate action, we must take into account not only character/personality *and* relevant situational factors, but also how character/personality and the situational factors interact to support or prohibit compassionate action.

Situational Barriers

According to psychological research, certain situational factors other than the number of others available to help are also important in constraining compassionate actions. In their famous and often cited *From Jerusalem to Jericho* study, Darley and Batson (1973) experimented with students at Princeton Theological Seminary. Participants arrived individually at a building and were given one of two messages (the first variable). One of the two messages required participants to give a presentation on the parable of the Good Samaritan. The other message required a presentation on the role and nature of ministering. After a short time to read the message, participants were instructed that owing to space, the presentations were to take place in another building. Participants were provided a map and given directions. However, participants were accorded different time-scales (the second variable, what Darley and Batson (1973, p. 104) refer to as 'hurry'). Those in the 'high-hurry' group were told they were running late, those in the 'intermediate-hurry' group were told to make their way over straight away, while those in the 'low-hurry' group were told that they were not needed for a short time, but to begin to make their way over. On leaving the initial room to make their way to the presentation room, participants walked through an alley in which a 'victim' 'was sitting slumped in a doorway, head down, eyes closed, not moving. As the subject went by, the victim coughed twice and groaned, keeping his head down' (Darely and Batson 1973, p. 104). Darley and Batson report that while one of the variables – the message – did not affect helping behaviour, the other – time – did. Those in less of a hurry were more likely to help (63 % or those in a low-hurry, 45 % in an intermediate-hurry and 10 % in a high-hurry). The conclusion here is that it was situational factors – in this case, time – which mattered and not the individual character of the participants.

Similar studies have also drawn the conclusion that dispositional factors may have little effect on helping actions (see, for example, Green et al. 1972;

cf. Clary and Miller 1986), while others have pointed to the importance of the perceptions held about those in need of help over and above character and dispositions. To this end, certain psychological studies report a positive correlation between helping behaviour and perceived similarity between those giving and receiving this help – in terms of their appearance (Piliavin et al. 1981), their perceived character (Weiner 1980) and their socio-political views (Ehlert et al. 1973).

So what are we to make of these psychological studies that point to situational factors – and not dispositions – as explaining altruism? According to philosopher Gilbert Harman our response should be to recognise that character traits and dispositions are not that useful in understanding helping behaviour. Following Ross (1977), Harman (1999) argues that attempts to explain helping behaviour in terms of dispositions are subject to a fundamental attribution error.[9] According to Harman (1999, p. 329),

> We very confidently attribute character traits to other people in order to explain their behaviour. But our attributions tend to be wildly incorrect and, in fact, there is no evidence that people differ in character traits. They differ in their situations and in their perceptions of their situations. They differ in their goals, strategies, neuoses, optimism, etc. But character traits do not explain what differences there are.

Contra Harman, I think there is good reason to be wary of conceiving any causal relationship between dispositions and helping behaviour as representing an attribution error. First, and as Clary and Miller (1986, p. 1359) suggest, there are some limitations to studies such as that conducted by Darley and Batson which 'consist of single, brief episodes of help'.[10] Clary and Miller's research findings suggest that participants whose helping behaviours had been nurtured over time (within the family, for example) or had been supported through recent engagement in highly cohesive groups exhibited a greater degree of sustained altruism and were less influenced by situational factors than those who either had not received this nurturing socialisation or had not participated in such groups.

In addition, there appears to be a more important reason for maintaining the importance of dispositions. It seems likely that situational factors can – and often do – impact on our helping behaviours, or to extend this, on our capacity in certain situations to be compassionate. Yet, even if it were psychologically possible, we would not want to discount the dispositional altogether. Indeed, the stronger the dispositions held the more likely it would seem that these can overcome structural/situational factors. While situational factors may explain why some do not undertake compassionate action, there are situations when actors are compassionate *in spite of* the existence of highly relevant and pressing situational factors which work to push them in other directions. Harman's account, then, is no argument against the existence of character traits per se, but rather it reminds us that 'the picture of moral development of the virtues is one of gradual development subject to set-backs in the face of extreme difficulty' (Athanassoulis 2000).

We can see this in operation amid the concerns around the standard of healthcare – and in particular the lack of compassionate care – in England. As considered in the introduction to this book, a dominant discourse surrounding concerns at nursing standards has been to identify a lack of compassionate care on behalf of healthcare professionals. Here, many have pointed to the fact that structural, logistical and practical factors – situational constraints, that is – prohibited the extent to which compassion could be demonstrated and enacted. Yet, while the various reports and studies interested in compassionate care generally do point to the existence of situational constraints acting on healthcare professionals working in the National Health Service, they do not paint a picture of a complete and universal lack of compassionate care. The Health Service Ombudsman (2011, p. 8) report which presents ten case studies demonstrating a lack of compassion points out that 'there are very many skilled staff within the NHS who provide a compassionate and considerate service to their patients'. That is, in spite of the general recognition of a range of situational constraints, many healthcare professional are still able to provide care for their patients in a compassionate way. Once again, situational factors appear less an argument against the importance of character traits, and more a reminder that certain constraints affect how character traits are enacted. This complex inter-relationship – and again the constraining workings of structural processes – is embodied in the following remarks from nurse, Maria Davison, on receipt of an award for compassionate care. For Davison (2015), 'frontline staff have the compassion within them to know what is right, they have the desire to do what is right, the competence to deliver what is right, yet the courage to challenge when things aren't right is often missing.' With this in mind, the crucial questions thus become how the situational and dispositional interact in ways which either serve to enable or limit expressions of compassion, and how compassion can be cultivated to a sufficient degree that structural processes are worked against (and indeed, we might add how can structural processes be changed to promote compassion).

The proper response therefore, as I understand it, is not to seek to accept or refute any of these individual studies and their findings in their entirety, but instead to identify their salient points so far as compassion is concerned. Certainly, taken collectively, the studies suggest that altruism and helping behaviour are complex and are affected by a range of factors, including those which are situationally specific – such as time, the number of possible helpers etc. Moreover, they serve as important reminders not only that compassion requires practical wisdom, but also of what sorts of contemplations practical wisdom so far as compassion is concerned requires. To return to the case of the seminary students at Princeton, it may simply have been that those in a high-hurry who did not stop to help the victim placed other prosocial attributes – compliance, wishing to please, sharing knowledge, punctuality, for example – over and above compassion in this situation. Similarly, it could be that, on reflection and where they to face an analogous situation in the near future, they would have acted differently, offering a more compassionate response to the victim. The core learning from such studies, it would seem to me, is not that situational factors trump the dispositional, but rather that they can impact upon them in particular and important ways.

Helplessness and Compassion Fatigue

In the introduction, and in light of the concept's (over) use in public and educational discourse, Henri Nouwen's contention that compassion is a hard virtue to practice was raised to bring into question the danger of viewing compassion as something wide-spread, easily accessible and akin to related pro-social behaviours, such as kindness or politeness, which while positive are better understood as representing something which stops short of compassion. Nouwen's reminder that compassion is hard and takes us to places we are likely to find uncomfortable points to two further, and related, barriers to compassion – helplessness and compassion fatigue.

When faced with the suffering of others, the task of challenging the causes of suffering and/or alleviating the suffering may simply be overwhelming. When we are told that the amount of suffering in the world today is higher than at any point since the end of the Second World War, our response may well be not to act to alleviate suffering where we see it. We may, instead, feel swamped and unable to act. We may lack the self-efficacy to believe that our actions will make a difference. Our response may be, 'how on earth can I make a difference given this amount of suffering?'. In other words, in the face of inordinate suffering, we may become a 'detached observer' (Boltanski 1999), unable to make sense of the suffering, its causes, its possible alleviation and, crucially, our agency in acting in respect of our compassion. Suffering, therefore, may engender what Wilkinson (2014, p. 121) refers to as 'a shared sense of powerlessness and moral inadequacy; for we routinely find that we have no adequate means to respond to the imperative of action that the brute facts of suffering impress on us'. This feeling of powerlessness can operate on different levels. We know from fields other than education that compassion can become hard(er) for those who have exhibited compassion frequently and consistently with regard to sufferers who are in close proximal relation. In short, when the demands of compassionate action are constant and relentless, they may lead to compassion fatigue.

The term 'compassion fatigue' was first used by Joinson (1992) with regard to the work of nurses, and is generally understood to refer to a state in which those acting in a caring role feel high levels of tension and stress by virtue of that role. Feelings associated with compassion fatigue include helplessness, anger and detachment. According to Figley (1995, p. 1) compassion fatigue can be understood as 'the cost of caring'. When subjects are involved in repeated situations requiring them to be compassionate, such requirements can take their toll, rendering the subject less able (or perhaps even unable) to be compassionate, reducing their feelings of self-efficacy. The challenges compassion brings can be significant. Speaking on BBC Radio Four's *Beyond Belief* programme, an aid worker with over 30-years experience working to support others, David Bainbridge (BBC 2015c), offered the following reflection on compassion fatigue in his work:

> I can think of one [example] that is very much in my memory from spending time in Goma in the Democratic Republic of Congo. Spending time with families who had fled their homes because of the atrocities that were being carried out, meeting survivors of rape, finding people living in the most basic shelter made of sticks and bamboo leaves, and sheltering whole families in this kind of temporary shelter in torrential rain and finding myself in my hotel at night under a mosquito net, just feeling a sense of despair, feeling

overwhelmed by the needs and finding it hard to really come to terms with just the extreme suffering, the depravity of the atrocities that I was hearing about, and finding it tempting to simply deny that it surely isn't as bad as their saying to try and shut it out.

In her work on compassion fatigue among nurses, Yoder (2010, p. 194) identifies three broad levels of compassion fatigue triggers. First are those triggers which stem from *caring for patients*, such as a sense of helplessness and stress. Second are *system issues*, such as workload pressures, time constraints and other associated systemic barriers. Third are a range of *personal issues* which impact on compassion fatigue, such as inexperience, and the nature of personal lives and histories. The nature of compassion fatigue is, of course, dynamic and relational. Those who experience compassion fatigue can, and do, seek out ways to lessen its effect. In Yoder's research, participants reported dialogue with others (peers or managers, for example) to be key mechanism in supporting their response to compassion fatigue.

Compassion, then, is challenging and can involve compassionate agents in contexts in which suffering is severe and relentless. In such circumstances, compassionate agents can become fatigued through the unremitting demands compassion can place upon them. Compassion fatigue is likely to affect only those who are involved in particular acute contexts requiring compassionate caring responses – such as healthcare workers, humanitarian aid workers and members of armed forces, for example (Yoder 2010). What relevance, though, does the concept of compassion fatigue have for the field of education?

In a book focusing on compassion in relation to the education and schooling of young people one must be wary of over- or misusing certain concepts. It seems unlikely that many educationalists or young people will be affected by compassion fatigue to the extent experienced by members of other professions. Nevertheless, I take there to be certain benefits for our understanding of compassion which can be tentatively drawn from an awareness and appreciation of literature on compassion fatigue. First, literature on compassion fatigue reinforces the contention that compassion involves, and is affected by, a range of complex and inter-related factors, including the respective roles/positions between the compassionate agent and the sufferer/s, significant situational and contextual factors, and intrapersonal factors acting on the agent. Second, the idea of compassion fatigue provides a warning for educationalists seeking to educate for compassion. A good deal of literature now exists on the (re) production of images of suffering found on news broadcasts, aid campaigns and fundraising marketing media in order to engender concern and compassion (Boltanski 1999; Moeller 1999; Kinnick et al. 2015). Though there is not an evidence base to suggest that this is the case, it would seem likely that some such media is played, shown and employed in schools and classrooms to engender awareness and support for the given issues at hand, within social studies/civics lessons or through fundraising activities, for example. Exposure to such media has a number of effects, and one is to desensitise receivers[11] (a form of compassion fatigue) (Boltanski 1999; Moeller 1999). Little is known about the use and effects of media representations of suffering in education, but we can at least posit that – and so far as compassion is concerned – educators need to pay some attention to the use and handling of such information in order to be aware of the possibilities for desensitisation and detachment which may result from over-use or exposure.

Conclusion

This chapter has examined the relationship between compassion and action. Building on the analysis of previous chapters, beneficent action has been understood as central to compassion. Compassionate action – as has been the case here – is typically conceived in terms of alleviating suffering, but can also comprise helping others to endure suffering. In addition, and while much less has been said here about compassionate action in this regard, compassion also plays a role in framing our judgements of others, judgements which may then be enacted as in the case of legal verdicts. With regard to alleviating responses, action has been presented as possessing a multitude of forms and possibilities, and a number of central questions which help to illuminate key features of these forms and possibilities have been identified. Once again, the use of deliberation and discernment central to practical wisdom has been identified as playing a crucial role in enabling compassionate agents to judge appropriate action responses. Understanding the ways in which caring and justice work through compassionate action has been posited as of fundamental importance. Finally, it has been suggested that no account of compassionate action can be considered complete without some discussion of significant barriers to compassionate action. To this end, certain barriers which can seek to constrain compassion have been examined and their implications for our understanding of compassion identified. Conceiving compassionate action as multifarious, complex and – at times – constrained is crucial to understanding not only the nature of compassion itself, but also compassion as it relates to education and schooling. These themes, therefore, are returned to in Chaps. 6 and 7.

NOTES

1. As opposed to governments, agencies etc.
2. I think we can also include here the perceptions of advocates acting directly on behalf of those suffering, but there is not space to fully justify and explore this here.
3. The analysis provided by Arnot et al. here is rather limited and they cite Christianity, Buddhism and Hume as leading proponents of the compassion as caring standpoint.
4. http://news.nd.edu/news/3728-notre-dames-tonelli-faced-horrors-of-bataan-refused-to-die/
5. It should be noted that these studies focus on volunteering which includes, but is not limited to, helping causes which seek to alleviate human suffering.
6. In their summary of data from the 2007 *Helping Out Survey* in England, Rochester et al. (2009, p. 126) report that (and we should remember that respondents could give more than one reason) 'just over half of current volunteers (53 per cent) in England indicated that a reason for getting involved was that they wanted to help people. Interestingly, the second most important reason was that "the cause was important to me" which was reported by 41 per cent of volunteers.... we might say that both of these could be described as value led (only 1 per cent however indicated it was to give something back'). But with 41 per cent also indicating that they wanted to meet people and make friends, the social aspect is important to...while 29 per cent said it was connected to the needs and interests of friends or family, and 21 per cent because family and friends did it'.
7. Participants, all university students, communicated by intercom on the pretence that this would avoid any embarrassment should sensitive subjects arise. Communicating in this way allowed the researchers to vary their instructions to participants regarding how many other participants were involved in the conversation. The seizure was conveyed by a researcher involved in the conversation altering their speech patterns and vocabulary in an obvious way.
8. See, for example, https://theconversation.com/the-21st-century-bystander-effect-happens-every-day-online-27496.
9. See John Doris (1998) for a further situationist account.

10. It should be noted that Clary and Miller do not make this point directly in relation to the study by Darley and Batson, but their point still holds in relation to that particular study.

11. Such a danger is a relatively common theme throughout accounts of compassion. Rousseau (1762/1979, p. 231), for example, argued that Émile 'must be touched and not hardened by the sight of human miseries. Long struck by the same sights, we no longer feel their impressions. Habit accustoms us to everything. What we see too much, we no longer imagine; and it is only imagination which makes us feel the ills of others'.

CHAPTER 5

Compassion and the Self

INTRODUCTION

To this point in this book, compassion has been presented as being largely other-regarding. When we come into relation with the suffering of others, we are moved to care for them, seek to understand them through empathic responses central to perspective sharing and follow some course of action appropriate to and guided by the situation of the other. For these reasons compassion relates primarily and in important ways to notions of beneficence, altruism, solidarity and care. Yet, at various times in the preceding chapters, notions of the self have been raised. It was argued in Chap. 2, for example, that a condition of compassion is the need to share similar possibilities with those whose suffering we come into contact with. As Nussbaum (2001, p. 408) suggests, through its intersubjectivity, compassion 'shows us something about our own lives: we see that we too are vulnerable to misfortune, that we are not any different from the people whose fate we are watching, and we therefore have some reason to fear a similar reversal'. These sentiments have their roots in Aristotle's principle of similar possibilities, and his views that a constituent part of compassion is that the suffering is such that 'one might expect it to befall ourselves or one of our friends, and moreover to befall us soon' (2012, p. 103; 1385b 13–16) and that in order to feel compassion 'we must obviously be capable of supposing that some evil may happen to us' (2012, p. 103; 1386a 28).

© The Author(s) 2017
A. Peterson, *Compassion and Education*,
DOI 10.1057/978-1-137-54838-2_5

In Chap. 3 it was discussed that the ways in which we conceive and position the self are essential to understanding the empathic distress necessary for compassion. Drawing on Hoffman's work on role-taking, it was suggested that not only could role-taking take two forms – self-focused and other-focused – but also that self-focused role-taking may well be problematic if it becomes one's sole focus (i.e. the tendency towards egoistic drift). It was further contended that this egoistic drift is not sufficient to deny the importance of self-focused role-taking completely given the empirical evidence that it can produce greater feelings of empathic distress than when other-focused role-taking is involved alone. On this basis, a case was made for the combination of self- and other-focused role-taking. In Chap. 4, comments were made about the relationship between self-efficacy and compassionate action, and it was argued that compassion and compassion fatigue are impacted in important ways by feelings of self-efficacy or lack of self-efficacy respectively.

These brief recaps signify not only that how we locate ourselves in relation to the other is important, but that so too is how we conceive and direct the self. That compassion relates to the self brings into focus the possibility that for all of its good intent compassion may involve some form of self-interest or egoism. Indeed, that compassion involves some form of concern for self could be viewed as something of an Achilles Heel. While this may be putting things rather strongly, identifying the existence of self-concern requires that something is said about what role this regard for self plays, and what form it takes, within compassion. The purpose of this chapter, therefore, is to take the challenge of self-regard seriously, and to argue that a positive regard for the self is a necessary part of compassion. With this in mind, the chapter explores different ways of conceiving regard for oneself in order to identify those specific aspects and readings of self-regard which we can understand to be conducive for compassion. Specifically, it will be argued that compassion can be understood as involving an enlightened and healthy approach to self which can be differentiated from more self-centred and egoistic forms. To make this argument, the chapter takes the following course. First, debates concerning Rousseau's distinction between *amour propre* and *amour de soi* are explored in order to shed some light on the ways in which a concern for self can be approached. The differences between *amour propre* and *amour de soi* are illustrative in building an understanding of what form negative and positive approaches to self might take. In the second section the focus shifts to a conception of self – framed as self-love – derived from

Aristotelian roots and which it is argued provides a useful approach for a positive reading of self-central to compassion. The focus of the third section is recent work in psychology on the concept of self-compassion. Here, some preliminary and tentative reflections are offered about the potential value and limitations of self-compassion to our understanding of compassion.

COMPASSION AND THE SELF– *AMOUR PROPRE* AND *AMOUR DE SOI*

As has been discussed previously, part of the power of compassion lies in its connecting of humans and human lives, bringing people into relationship with each other in a sympathetic, caring and empathic way. That this is so, and as suggested in the introduction to this chapter, means that compassion relates to conceptions of self and necessarily requires us to think about whether some conceptions of the self are more apt for compassion than others. While some concept of self is central to our conceptions of compassion, this raises questions about whether and how concern for self can be said to complement or detract from compassion's altruism and beneficence. At a general level, the need to engage with such questions can be readily illustrated. Let us say Nigel is low in confidence and holds a very negative understanding of himself. It would seem likely that how Nigel regards himself will impact in important ways on how the extent to which he can be compassionate for others. We might say something similar, though for different reasons, about the likely impact of Simon's arrogance, self-interest and status-seeking concept of self for his ability to show compassion for others. There seem, then, to be important issues at play between the ways in which we conceive and care for ourselves and the extent to which we empathise and care for others. In this section my aim is to demonstrate some fundamental issues relating to notions of the self by examining debates about the self which have arisen from Rousseau's account of *pitié*. These debates provide some conceptual groundwork which not only helps to illuminate some of the key tensions involved, but also provides a platform for the sections which follow.

To start with, let us recap some important general points Rousseau makes in relation to *pitié* and the self. In Chap. 3 it was identified that the relationship between social and individual benefit is central to Rousseau's principle of *pitié*. In his Discourse on Inequality Rousseau (1755/2009, p. 53) presents *pitié* as 'a natural sentiment moderating the action of self-love in each individual and so contributing to the mutual preservation of the whole species'. Here, *pitié* is understood as playing a regulatory role so far as love of oneself is concerned. In Èmile, Rousseau provides further development of his ideas in this area, and positions self-love as anterior to all passions.[1] As also discussed in previous chapters, Rousseau situates the learning of *pitié* as crucial for Èmile's moral and social development, and does so in ways which could be read as prioritising Èmile's growth over and above the needs and goals of those suffering – or at least does so in ways which place some importance on self-interest.

Different readings of Rousseau's account are available, and these point to contested interpretations of the relationship between *pitié* and self-interest. In his commentary, Marks (2007, p. 728) understands Rousseau's position as one in which compassion does not oppose self-interest, but 'is among those modifications of self-love that are good for us and for others'. On this reading, compassion moderates love for self and plays a vital social function in working to bring us into community with others. Others, however, have been more critical. In her reading of Rousseau's *Émile*, Faulkner (2014a) directs her criticism toward the notion that bringing students (in Rousseau's case Émile) into relation with suffering is not solely, or even mainly, about alleviating this suffering. Rather, viewing the suffering of others is beneficial precisely *for the student.* The force of this criticism lies in the extent to which those who are suffering are instrumentalised, treated that is as means towards the ends of the students. Of particular relevance is Rousseau's claims in *Émile* (1755/2009, p. 224) that 'one pities in others only those ills from which one does not feel oneself exempt' and that 'pity is sweet, because, when we put ourselves in the place of one who suffers, we are aware nevertheless of the pleasure of not suffering like him'. Faulkner (2014a, p. 145; emphasis in original) suggests that

> The object of Émile's education, however, is a *particular response to suffering* rather than its alleviation. Suffering is a resource for Émile's affective and moral training, and as important a lesson as learning to feel is the maintenance of a distance from misfortune.

A similar stance is adopted by White (2008, p. 36), who argues that 'the basic problem is that Rousseau attempts to link compassion to self-interest, and this creates a tension between altruism and self-love that cannot be easily resolved'. According to White (2008, p. 37), through his commitment to positioning the pitier as viewing those suffering as 'worse off' and as gaining pleasure from understanding that it is not oneself who is suffering, Rousseau's *pitié* appeals 'to our own sense of superiority'. Moreover, White contends that when notions of self-love and compassion come into conflict, the former 'always trumps' the latter (2008, p. 40).

To understand these points in relation to Rousseau's account – and indeed subsequent readings of it – we need to appreciate the distinction he draws in his *Discourses* between *amour de soi* and *amour propre* – a distinction which is also useful for developing an understanding of what might constitute a positive notion of self-interest as part of compassion. Rousseau presents *amour de soi* as a natural, self-preserving capacity which is guided by reason, can be modified by pity, and which serves to develop one's humanity and virtue. Most subsequent interpretations understand *amour de soi* as including self-preservation and well-being, but going beyond this to include reflecting on what such well-being consists of, and how this might be attained[2] (Kolodny 2010). According to Rousseau (1762/1979, p. 213) 'we have to love ourselves to preserve ourselves; and it follows immediately from the same sentiment that we love what preserves us'. So far as *amour de soi* is concerned, this is a self-love which involves 'gentle and affectionate passions' (214).

In contrast, *amour propre* is an artificial attribute developed through social interactions and which inherently involves a feeling of superior regard for oneself over others. With *amour propre* there is an important sense in which the individual is seeking to develop their status with respect to how they are regarded by others, whether or not this regard is accurate,[3] and how they stand relative to others. In other words, and so far as *amour propre* is concerned, the self is not only relative to others but is also at least in part constituted by the views of others (Bertram 2010).

In his interpretation, Nicholas Dent (1988, 1998) understands Rousseau's *pitié* as acting to *mediate* the effects of *amour propre*. On this basis, Dent (1998) suggests that *amour propre* thus requires direction rather than suppression. To develop this argument Dent (1998, p. 61) accepts that unrestrained *amour propre* involves a particular psychological issue for the self, given that the agent feels that:

his 'person' – the figure he cuts, the differential reception he is afforded – matters above all else, an individual neglects even the elementary needs of human well-being and happiness, and transfers his sense of self-worth, the meaning and value of his being and life, to the verdict that the regard others pay him reveals in respect of the estimate of his importance they hold.

When this form of *amour propre* is at play, the importance placed on the regard of others is not only pervasive, but demanding and unending. In short, and as Kolodny (2010, p. 171) suggests, 'inflamed amour-propre cannot be satisfied'.

In the face of this psychological challenge, which can only lead to 'our own ruin, to the destruction of humane intercourse and life with others, and into a condition where we shall be subject to the most frightful of abuses', and in contrast to most readings, Dent (1998, p. 63) suggests that rather than constricting or subduing *amour propre*, social life can include a recognition of *amour propre* without befalling to its malign influences. This step is based on shifting our understanding of what it is precisely that gives us status and regard from others. In this way, Dent's accommodation of *amour propre* involves a crucial step. This is to argue that the highest regard and status one can gain from one's fellows is being a fellow man – one who is concerned about his fellow men. On this reading correctly framed *amour propre* tempers the need for status through the recognition of others.

For Dent, once we accept that the highest status we can have from others comes from being a social, beneficent person *amour propre* can be understood as playing a crucial regulatory role to this end. A crucial distinction in this form of argument is that while unhealthy *amour propre* focuses on the desire for moral superiority over others, its healthy form rests on moral equality (Kolodny 2010). In support of his argument, Dent (1998, p. 67) draws on the role played by *pitié* in moving us towards the proper relationship between humans, citing the following passage from *Émile* (1762/1979, p. 244):

> He is a man; he is interested in his brothers; he is equitable; he judges his peers... He pities these miserable kings, slaves of all that obey them. He pities these false wise men, chained to their vain reputation. He pities these rich fools, martyrs to their display.

On this reading, it is through sentiments such as *pitié* that humans become aware of, and extend toward, others.[4] That is, and because suffering is a feature of human existence, *pitié* helps us to understand the humanity in others and, as a result, brings us into relation with the conditions of others.[5]

In contrast to Dent's more positive reading of the possible relationship between *amour propre*, *pitié* and regard from others, some have offered a solely negative reading of the principle. Chazan (1993, p. 341) reads Rousseau as arguing that *amour propre* has 'no rightful place in our lives at all'. Rather than being open to the positive reading and role involved in Dent's account, Chazan understands Rousseau to be advocating *amour propre's* 'obliteration . . . together with the kind of self-conception held by a person under its influence'. Central here, and unlike Dent, is the more standard view that the vanity and self-servingness which characterises *amour propre* produce a *wholly* negative condition; one which corrupts humans from the self-love of *amour de soi* found in our natural state, upon which we can become dependent, and in which the competitive and comparative gaze of others plays a crucial role in actually constituting our conception of the self. *Amour propre*, that is, is a false self – and one which restricts our ability to show compassion for others. The cure, according to Chazan's commentary of Rousseau, is not to find a more positive reconciliation of *amour propre*, but rather to recover the more positive conception of self associated with *amour de soi*. It is a restoration of self which is required, one which for some involves recognising and appreciating the mutual bond between individual interests and those of the collectivity – or for Rousseau the general will – through one's participation as a moral and political citizen.[6] For Chazan (1993, p. 345), this requires that the self

> must move from the dependencies, comparisons and illusions of amour-propre to the authenticity of 'what really is' . . . it must become a being that has a non-comparative conception of who and what it is, a self-determining being whose sense of its own existence and worth is independent of public opinion. It must become an autonomous, self-legislating, rational citizen, one capable of acting on principle.

On this reading, the virtuous self and the self constituted by the esteem and regard of others are not compatible.

In his consideration of Rousseau's views of compassion, Richard White offers a slightly different analysis. For White (2008, p. 46), while Rousseau 'shows how this form of self-love (or *amour propre*) can be channelled – or sublimated – through the education of compassion . . . it is still a very peculiar kind of compassion which remains self-involved even while it claims to be other-directed'. Central to White's argument appears to the belief that self-interest is fatally problematic for any meaningful conception of compassion. From this perspective, which has its roots in theological commitments, compassion becomes troubled when it is viewed as a 'conditional good and not as a final goal' (White 2008, p. 46). Thus, for White (2008, p. 40), who draws on Buddhist perspectives, compassion should be 'oriented towards self-overcoming'.

Unlike White, I do not believe that the view that compassion is not selfless is either fatal or, actually, that it even detracts from compassion. Indeed, there is a good deal of support from proponents of compassion that some sense of self-regard is not only acceptable for compassion, but may even play a necessary part of it. Such a reading is found within a range of perspectives on compassion.[7] It was suggested in the last chapter, and for example, that empirical studies suggest in actual practice that those engaged in compassionate actions such as 'volunteers...for instance, do not distinguish systematically between egoistic and altruistic motives' (Dekker and Halman 2003, p. 4). In a study of the relationship between self-interest and altruism in the United States, Wuthnow (1991, p. 22) found that 'being intensely committed to self-realization and material pleasure did not seem to be incompatible with doing volunteer work... People who were the most individualistic were also the most likely to value doing things to help others'. These empirical findings find some support in theoretical literature. In his contemporary account of virtues, Comte-Sponville (2003, p. 113) argues that compassion may well involve some form of egoism for the extent to which it involves both self-focused role-taking and similar possibilities, but contends that some form of self-interest is found within a range of virtues (such as generosity and love, for instance). On this basis, and for this reason, compassion 'is real and no less...for perhaps not being selfless'. On this account – one which I would agree with – the fact that compassion involves some form of self-interest is not in and of itself fatal.

As the discussion of Rousseau's work on *amour propre* and *amour de soi* makes clear, there are a number of different ways of conceiving self-interest. As we have seen, when self-interest is constituted by one's status vis-à-vis others and one's economic, political or moral superiority over others, we have clear and pertinent cause for concern. Similarly, if by self-interest we mean that we are guided only by (or perhaps even largely by) our own interests and either ignore or, worse still, subjugate the interests of others to further our own ends, then clearly, again, this is an issue. These ruminations mean that we need to say something further and more specific about the precise and proper relationship between regard for self and compassion. The next section seeks to respond to this need by exploring discussions on Aristotelian self-love. It will be argued that we surely *do* have at least some interest in ourselves, our lives, our own goals and our relationships in life with others. It will be contended that rather than seeing these as inimical for compassion, a more appropriate focus is how these interests are brought into relation with and mediated by our concern for others.

ARISTOTELIAN SELF-LOVE

What form, then, might a positive concern for self take – one that not only provides more substantive detail than Rosseau's principle of *amour de soi* but also provides resonance for compassion? The aim of this section is to explore particular way of framing this positive concern for self and to suggest that certain approaches to caring for, and valuing, oneself – approaches that is which are rooted in Aristotelian notions of positive self-love and understanding – appear more akin to compassion than other forms of self-interest which prioritise the self over others through forms of unhealthy competitiveness, narcissism, superiority and/or self-aggrandisement relative to others. In order to do this the nature of Aristotelian self-love is examined and it is suggested that viewing self-love from an Aristotelian perspective provides a number of important insights and, as such, helps us to clarify what form a positive regard for oneself relevant for compassion might take.

While Aristotle does not present us with a full psychological account of the virtuous self (Homiak 1981; Owens 1988), what he has to say about love for the self and the positioning of the self in relation to others – as for example in relation to friendship – provides some important reflections for our focus on compassion and its connection to self. The first point to make here is that love of oneself is, for Aristotle, crucial for our love of others and for virtue. In the Nichomachean Ethics, Aristotle positions self-love in relationship to friendship, and to understand his account we must, first, consider what it means for someone to be a friend. Aristotle (2009, p. 168; 1166a) defines a friend by identifying a number of features. First, a friend is one 'who wishes and does what is good . . . for the sake of his friend'. Second, a friend is one who 'wishes his friend to exist and live, for his own sake'. Third and fourth, a friend is defined by others as one 'who lives with and ... has the same tastes as another'. Fifth, a friend is one who 'grieves and rejoices with his friend'. These elements of friendship established, Aristotle draws the connection to self by suggesting that 'each of these is true of the good man's relationship to himself'.[8] In other words, the same sorts of capacities and desires we attribute to others when friendship is involved, we attribute to ourselves when self-love is involved (what Harcourt (2011, p. 85) refers to as the same-relation constraint).

In further defining self-love, Aristotle offers two contrasting approaches. Self-love – and Aristotle understood this to be its common meaning, reflecting its prevalence in society – can refer to a reproachable sentiment to oneself by which one seeks wealth, gratification, recognition and bodily pleasures (in this sense it bears some similarities with Rousseau's *amour propre*). A more positive form of self-love is involved when we seek those things which are most noble, and desire to act justly in respect of the common good and in accordance with the virtues. That is, a 'virtuous person is one with the right kind of self-love' (Chazan 1998, p. 63; emphasis added). For this reason, a lover of self adopting this second form benefits not just themselves, but also others.[9]

On Aristotle's account, then, when we are virtuous, and love the good, we are in a position to love others – crucially – in a positive sense. To love oneself involves processes of knowing *and* becoming aware. That is, while we may know those features and characteristics which comprise us, we also hold open the possibility that we may be mistaken about who we are and so seek to understand our *real* selves (Kristjánsson 2010; some further comments are made about this distinction between the perceived and real self in the next section). Moreover, and partly for this reason, a close relationship exists between self-love and practical wisdom. That is, someone who exhibits practical wisdom can also be considered to be one who holds a positive form of love for themselves (Homiak 1981; Harcourt 2011). In her Aristotelian account of the psychology of the virtuous self, Homiak (1981, p. 638) presents a number of features which illustrate this connection between love for self and practical wisdom. To start with, Homiak draws on Aristotle's various contentions – (1) that through our actions we express ourselves, (2) that we love those activities which enable us to reach our potential and (3) that the most important human action involves planning our lives – to argue that to love oneself involves being a 'rational planner'. Homiak further claims that rational planning is far from being simply a straightforward or logistical process. Rather it requires the formulation and reformulation of plans towards a given end. For this reason, rational planning encompasses an *eudaimonistic* judgement concerning one's own flourishing and recurring reflection about how such flourishing may be attained.

The virtuous person who loves themselves in the Aristotelian positive sense is, then, a rational planner – one who chooses the virtuous life because they plan rationally with an eudaimonistic judgement in mind. To accept this line of argument carries with it three further important points for our understanding of self-love and compassion. First, the moral agent who possesses the right character and acts with virtuous conduct gains pleasure from doing so at least in part because those actions are expressions of themselves. This claim not only brings further clarity to our understanding of self-love, but is significant to our general understanding of the ways in which compassion brings us into relation with others. If we recall from Chap. 2, it was argued that on the account I am seeking to provide our mutual relationships to others (in compassion's case, those who are suffering) is based on notions of love, care and virtue rather than conforming to some form of duty derived from law. Thus, the question 'why should I show compassion?' is better responded to along the lines of 'because I am/desire to be a particular sort of person' rather than 'because I am following a certain rule' or 'because I am fulfilling my duties'. Now, it seems to me that the first sort of response is more able to understand particular dispositions – in this case compassion – as an expression of the self. While it may be possible to suggest that fulfilling ones duties by following a rule could constitute an expression self, this would be a rather limited sense of self. Second, the relationship between self-love and virtuous actions is a causal one in a particular direction. That is, self-love leads to virtue and is 'not the end for which virtuous actions are done' (Homiak 1981, p. 640). This is an important recognition not only for the extent to which positive self-love supports virtuous actions, but also because it necessarily means that those without love for themselves are unable to act virtuously. Third, and at the level of individual and specific virtues, there exists a reciprocal relationship between self-love and the virtues. That is, and for example, a compassionate person is a self-lover and a self-lover is compassionate.[10] Taken together, these three points highlight that when conceived as a virtue in the Aristotelian sense, compassion is simultaneously good for the self and for others (Carr 1991).

To conclude this section, it is without doubt that an interest or concern for oneself can take negative forms. For those who seek to develop a meaningful conception of compassion, this raises two particular challenges. The first is to consider whether compassion is best regarded as selfless or as incorporating some form of self-interest. The argument made so far in this chapter has been that compassion is not selfless, and that this requires some consideration as to how regard for the self can be accommodated within compassion. It has been suggested that positive forms of regard for self are not only possible but can be viewed as holding a mutually beneficial relationship with compassion. It is this relationship which is central to the Aristotelian conception of self-love examined here. In the next section, our focus changes to an approach to conceiving the self which has not only gained a good deal of attention in psychological fields over the last 10 years but is of particular relevance to compassion; namely, the concept of *self-compassion*.

SELF-COMPASSION

Speaking on BBC Radio Four's *Women's Hour* about the possibility of teaching compassion and empathy to children, education consultant Nikkola Daniel (2013; emphasis added) suggested that

> We are not particularly skilled at being *compassionate towards ourselves*... There is a tendency to think that compassion is all about extending towards others, but it is just as much about showing love and kindness towards ourselves, which is the starting point.

Similar sentiments are not uncommon in the literature on compassion. Karen Armstrong (2011, pp. 76–77), for example, argues that

> Before you can embrace the whole world you must focus on yourself... notice how much peace, happiness and benevolence you possess already... Next, become conscious of your anger, fear and anxiety. Look deeply into the seeds of rage within yourself. Bring to mind some of your past suffering and the pleasure in things we all tend to take for granted. Finally, look at yourself with even-mindedness. You are not unique... You have failings but you also have talents.

While there may be some good reasons to accept the sentiment expressed by Daniel and Armstrong, precisely what it means to *show compassion* toward oneself needs some unpicking. In her comments, Daniel makes two slightly different points. One is that we can show love and kindness towards ourselves (which is not in and of itself different from the arguments made in the previous section). The second and potentially differentiated claim is that we can actually *show compassion to ourselves*. This leads us to question whether self-love and self-compassion are synonymous and, whether compassionate self-love is the same or is different to the Aristotelian account discussed above. With this in mind, the focus of this section is on recent work in psychology which has offered the concept of *self-compassion*. Through an examination of self-compassion, it will be suggested that certain themes central to the concept are noteworthy for those interested in compassion for the extent to which they bear *some* similarities and differences to Aristotelian accounts. Given the lack of current attention paid to self-compassion within educational literature, the arguments provided in this section are tentative, and – it is hoped – will prompt further discussion and research.

Over the last 15 years, self-compassion has been identified as providing a meaningful and useful psychological concept. According to Neff and Germer (2013, p. 28), self-compassion comprises 'three interacting components: self-kindness versus self-judgement, a sense of common humanity versus isolation, and mindfulness versus over-identification when confronting painful self-relevant thoughts and emotions'. Some studies suggest that self-compassion enables the agent to engage with the self's negative aspects and experiences without doing so in an overly judgemental manner (see, e.g., Marshall et al. 2015). In other words, when we are self-compassionate we treat ourselves with a degree of humility and care which while not ignoring judgements seeks a degree of acceptance or kindness toward ourselves. To this end, Germer and Neff (2013) distinguish self-compassion from self-pity, viewing the latter as involving a '"woe is me" attitude in which people become immersed in their own problems and forget that others have similar problems'.[11]

For its proponents, self-compassion is understood as being a more useful approach to the relationship to oneself than that provided, for example, by other concepts – notably self-esteem (for an overview, see Neff and Vonk 2009; for a critical overview of research on self-esteem see Baumeister et al. 2003). Crucial here is that, through mindfulness and self-kindness, self-compassion inherently involves *caring* for oneself over and above merely having confidence in one's ability, which may or may not be justified, or indeed holding oneself in esteem. Self-compassion is therefore presented by its proponents as avoiding some of the excessive pitfalls associated with self-esteem, such as narcissism, competitiveness with others and risk-taking. Though more is said specifically about education in the last two chapters, it is worth briefly noting here that this element of self-compassion literature (i.e. the focus on *caring* for oneself) is of educational significance not least because, and somewhat surprisingly given its critical treatment in psychological and educational literature, the importance of developing pupils' self-esteem remains a fairly common refrain in educational circles.[12]

A further point of interest for our consideration of compassion is the extent to which, while focusing on the self, self-compassion embraces one's connections to others. In this sense, self-compassion is presented as involving a 'connected mindset that is inclusive of others', bringing one into relation with human experience. As Neff and Germer (2013, p. 29) report, 'self-compassion connects one's flawed condition to the shared human condition, so that features of the self are considered from a broad, inclusive perspective'. This recognition and appreciation of common humanity is central to self-compassion, moving the agent (in this case the suffering agent) away from a sole focus on their own, personal suffering and positioning their circumstances within a wider conception of human fragility. According to proponents of self-compassion, appreciating common humanity can serve to remind the sufferer that they are not suffering alone or indeed are alone in their suffering. In this way, the self is brought into relation with others through focusing on those states, worries, capacities and goals we share, hold in common, and which connect us rather than focusing on those things we do not share or which isolate us from others.

Given the significance of common humanity to compassion, its central presence within self-compassion is not inconsequential. What is more, there is some evidence to suggest that those with high levels of self-compassion demonstrate greater levels of prosocial attitudes towards others. One study reports that those who demonstrate higher levels of self-compassion evidence 'more empathetic concern, altruism, perspective taking, and forgiveness' (Neff and Pommier 2012), while Heffernan et al. (2010) also report a positive connection between self-compassion and compassion for others. While further research and reflection is necessary to examine further the precise nature and strength of the relationship between self-compassion and compassion for others, such findings are noteworthy and are certainly not inconsequential for how we conceive the self in relation to compassion.

Now, at this stage, it is both necessary and important to establish some provisos. First, while those advocating self-compassion are keen to suggest that self-compassion can be taught through mindfulness programmes, the research evidence currently in existence is derived mainly from interventions with adults. Though there is some research evidence regarding developing self-compassion with adolescents (see, for example, Bluth and Blanton 2014), the existing research base is presently extremely limited. Second, and as a result, there has been very little critical examination of the suitability and application of self-compassion in relation to the education and schooling of young people. To repeat an important point – further research is needed before any firmer conclusions are possible. Yet, and with these provisos remembered, there does seem to be at least a prima facie case for considering the extent to which self-compassion may be a useful construct for those concerned with educating for compassion.

So, while recognising the currently limited evidence base for self-compassion as a basis for educational interventions with young people, of what possible value may the concept be to our understanding of self as it relates to compassion? One way of approaching this question – one which I think is instructive for our tentative purposes – is to position certain features of self-compassion against other approaches to understanding the self. In seeking to do this in what remains of this chapter, it should be noted that the term being used here is self-understanding rather than self-love. I take self-understanding to be a related, though wider concept to self-love. It is a concept which – as will hopefully become clear – is more apt to the analysis I wish to provide here, though I will bring us back more specifically to self-love towards the end of the section.

The contrast drawn by Kristján Kristjánsson between Aristotelian and positive-psychological conceptions of self-understanding seems a particularly helpful framework for the task at hand. This distinction is framed in relation to how one approaches the concept of self. Kristjánsson thus distinguishes between the self as understood by Aristotle and the self as understood by positive psychologists. For Aristotle (and as we have seen in relation to self-love) the self comprises 'the set of characteristics that truly make us what we are, whether we are aware of it or not', while in contrast for positive psychology, the self is the 'set of beliefs and attitudes (feelings/commitments) that we hold in relation to ourselves' (2010, p. 181). While I think it would be too strong to suggest that self-compassion *necessarily* takes as its focus the true self (which we may or may not know), in its commitment to mindfulness and our relationships to others, including how we are other-regarding, self-compassion does seem to be interested in engaging with the real self and thus mediating any gap between our self as it really is and our (perhaps mistaken) perceptions of the self.[13]

Kristjánsson (2010, p. 189) identifies various other features of self-understanding around which differences between Aristotelian self-understanding and positive psychological accounts of self-understanding can be drawn: 'the self to be known', 'the self's relationship to value', 'the process of self-understanding', 'the value of self-change', 'emotions following self-understanding' and 'the ultimate goals of self-understanding'. The two accounts conceive each of these categories in different ways. So, and for example, with regard to the self to be known, Aristotelian self-understanding 'comprises the character states that one actually possesses', from which one can grow, with the self socially embedded. In contrast, positive-psychological self-understanding is a thinner, individualised 'choosing self'. Similarly, whereas Aristotelian self-understanding seeks to connect to an 'objective, inter-human reality', the positive-psychological account the self chooses the good to be desired and sought, subject to the constraint of non-interference with the goods chosen by others.

Of particular interest to our focus here, is that both of these features – social embeddedness and inter-human reality – are features which are posited as central to self-compassion by its proponents. Crucially, so too is another of the features. This is the extent to which self-understanding on the Aristotelian reading involves both pleasant and painful emotions, with the latter providing the moral agent with an opportunity to learn and grow. We have seen above that a core principle of self-compassion is the extent to which self-compassion involves the agent in engaging with the self's negative aspects and experiences without doing so in an overly judgemental manner. Understanding one's suffering in an appropriate manner involves seeking a path between underplaying the seriousness of the suffering (flippant dismissiveness, or denial, for example) and allowing one's understanding to become destructive (wallowing in self-pity, for example).

However, and here we have a sense of caution about the potential commensurability between self-compassion and a stronger sense of self-love akin to an Aristotelian approach, it is not clear what the *ultimate goal* of self-compassion's understanding of self is. As Kristjánsson (2010, p. 190) suggests, on the Aristotelian account the goal of self-understanding is both an 'appreciation of truth and...a self-respect in which the mature self has learnt to respect itself as the possessor or moral and other truths', while on the positive psychological account the aim is 'psychological effectiveness and self-esteem'. Here we have an important ambiguousness about which proponents of self-compassion are yet to fully attend. On the one hand, and as we have seen, proponents place little store by self-esteem, yet on the other they appear more concerned with self-compassion as a psychologically effective concept than they do with notions of morality and the true self (aside, in fairness, to its potential to enhance the capacity for prosocial behaviours, though this remains something more of an identified outcome with some evidence than a substantive claim supported by a range of evidence). To my knowledge, no supporter of self-compassion has developed an account in which its ultimate goal is truth and moral – as opposed to solely psychological – self-understanding.

Now, the tentative claim I am making here is certainly not that Aristotelian self-understanding and self-compassion are synonymous. Rather, I am seeking to make the more modest suggestion that to some extent (and with the proviso made above about the vagueness of its ultimate goal) self-compassion seems to embody a thicker, more socially embedded approach to the self than those typically found within positive psychology and thus may offer something to educationalists and philosophers interested in compassion. We might, then, understand self-compassion as a particular sub-category of self-concept – one which seemingly bears some relation to self-understanding in that it involves particular ideas about knowing the self, valuing the self and of emotions concerned with self-understanding. We might also suggest that there is something in self-compassion – its emphasis on valuing and caring for the self and on kindness – which speaks to positive notions of self-love, That is, for self-compassion our value comes from ourselves and positive relations *with* others rather than our status *against, at the expense of, or in positions of, superiority to* others.

CONCLUSION

Compassion requires us to recognise, come into relation with, and care for others. It has been argued in this chapter that, in doing so and in order to bring compassion about, compassion is not selfless but requires us to hold some form of positive self in relation to ourselves. How we conceive ourselves is, of course, complex and impacted upon by a range of factors. For both Aristotle and Rousseau, for example, forms of self-interest can – and often are – corrupted by social processes and engagements. People can, for example, come to prioritise selfishness and the furtherance of their own status and standing over others – whether financial, political, social or, indeed, moral. That this is so and is often the form which a concern for self takes should not be read as being the only form of self available to us. More positive forms of self-love such as those favoured by the Aristotelian accounts discussed here, hold out the possibilities for a deeper and more caring sense of self, ones related to *eudaimonistic* judgements about both our own lives and those of others. It has also been contended here that not only are these forms of self-love essential for our own well-being, they are also important for our relationships – including relationships involving compassion – with others. When we hold a positive form of love for ourselves our actions become expressions of ourselves, with self-love a key process in the pathway to virtue. In other words, and to put it in simple terms, compassion for others and love for self are mutually constitutive: to show the sort of love for others necessary for compassion, we need to love ourselves.

NOTES

1. 'The source of our passions, the origin and the principle of all the others, the only one born with man and which never leaves him so long as he lives is self-love – a primitive, innate passion, which is anterior to every other, and of which all others are in a sense only modifications' (1762/1979, pp. 212–213).
2. Kolodny (2010, p. 173) identifies both a preservative and reflective form of *amour de soi*.
3. The importance of accurate evaluations is highlighted, in particular, by Kolodny (2010).
4. Dent (1998, p. 67) references the following argument to further support this position: 'So long as his [Emilé's] sensibility remains limited to his own individuality, there is nothing moral in his actions. It is only when it begins to extend outside of himself that it takes on, first, the sentiments and, then, the notions of good and evil which truly constitute him as a man and an integral part of his species' (1762/1979, pp. 219–220).
5. Adam Smith appealed to the notion of 'self-command', by which he meant the ability for humans to regulate their selfish intentions and to focus instead on the good of society (Lamb 1974). For Smith (1759/2009, p. 73) the 'disposition to admire, and almost to worship, the rich and the powerful, and to despise, or, at least, to neglect persons of poor and mean condition...is...the great and most universal cause of the corruption of our moral sentiments'. In order to avoid such corruption we must bring into line our own conceptions of self with how we appear to others.

6. While solutions to unhealthy *amour propre* may involve both an individual and collective remedy, commentators are divided as to whether *amour propre* is solely an individual concern or whether there is also a collective form of self which can attain the regard of others for the collectivity (see Kolodny 2010 for an exploration). Dent (1988, 1998) provides a leading example of position which views *amour propre* as only an individual property.

7. That compassion requires some sense of valuing the self, has some theological basis, as is illustrated in the following contemplation provided by the Dalai Lama (2003, p. 125): 'for someone to develop genuine compassion towards others, first he or she must have a basis upon which to cultivate compassion, and that basis is the ability to connect to one's own feelings and to care for one's own welfare... Caring for others requires caring for oneself'.

8. Aristotle (2009, p. 170; 1166a) denies that these feelings of friendship can occur in instances where a man is bad because 'there is nothing in him to love; so that if to be thus is the height of wretchedness, we should strain every nerve to avoid wickedness and should endeavour to be good; for so and only so can one be either friendly to oneself or a friend to another'.

9. 'Those, then, who busy themselves in an exceptional degree with noble actions all men approve and praise; and if all were to strive towards what is noble and strain every nerve to do the noblest of deeds, everything would be for the common weal, and everyone would secure for himself the goods that are greatest, since virtue is the greatest of goods' (Aristotle 2009, p. 175; 1169a; emphasis in original).

10. Homiak explores and justifies this second point in relation to two virtues – courage and temperance – but if accepted it can be understood to apply to all virtues.

11. Emerging evidence also suggests that self-compassion is positively connected to lower anxiety and depression (Neff 2012; Neff and Germer 2013) as well as less fear of failure (Neff 2003; Neff and Germer 2013).

12. In England, see Personal, Social and Health Education Association 2015; DfE 2016 for recent examples. Interestingly, in Australia there has been something of a curricular move away from self-esteem towards the wider concept of self-worth.

13. On this point Neff and Vonk (2009) argue that 'self-compassion... is not a particular type of self-evaluation or cognitive representation of the self. Rather, it is an open-hearted awareness that can embrace all aspects of personal experience'. This seems to stop short of the connection to truth and moral worth central to Aristotelian self-understanding.

CHAPTER 6

Teaching about and for Compassion: Pedagogical Connections

INTRODUCTION

The term 'compassion' has found expression within various educational texts and curricular initiatives for civic and moral education across a number of jurisdictions over the last two decades. In Australia, for example, the Values Education Program, for example, developed as part of the *National Framework for Values Education in Australian Schools*, cited 'care and compassion' – defined as 'care for oneself and others' – as one of nine values to be promoted and taught in schools (Australian Government, 2005). In the current Australian Curriculum, compassion represents a value to be explored through both the subject Civics and Citizenship and through the General Capability of Ethical Understanding. In England, the explicit teaching of compassion has gained some important attention and traction within various documents and guides produced by the Jubilee Centre for Character and Virtues at the University of Birmingham and appears in various curricular materials (see, e.g., Arthur et al. n.d.; and, http://www.jubileecentre.ac.uk/userfiles/jubileecentre/pdf/TaughtCourse/WDS/Resource_21.pdf), and alongside this current book there seems to be a growing attention to the teaching of compassion in and through education (see, e.g., Coles 2015a; Felderhof and Thompson 2014). Perhaps more commonly – and certainly too common to cite instances here – key features of compassion, such as care, empathy and altruism, are often found in the intentions and curricular of educational systems and schools across jurisdictions. While I take it, therefore, to be uncontroversial to say that notions such as care, empathy

© The Author(s) 2017
A. Peterson, *Compassion and Education*,
DOI 10.1057/978-1-137-54838-2_6

and altruism are core intentions of educational practice and discourse, it remains a further matter what precise meanings are attached to these terms as well as – for the present analysis – how and whether they are positioned in relation to the cultivation of compassion.

Aside from these conceptual and definitional questions, we should also remember that it is, of course, one thing to state the importance (educational and otherwise) of compassion and its component terms, and quite another to provide a clear and convincing programme for its cultivation in schools. As the foregoing chapters have hopefully suggested, nurturing compassion opens up a realm of possibilities (not to say challenges!) for schools and teachers, not least how we conceive compassion in the first place. My intention in this chapter is to draw on the analysis provided in previous chapters, as well as recent work in the field of character education, in order to offer some possible ways through which compassion and its central components might be educated in schools. While I hope that the contentions offered here are of *some* practical value, they will only be as such if they are taken up, refined and appropriated in ways shaped by the particular contexts in which educators work and young people live.

Following this introduction, the chapter comprises three sections. In the first section some basic comments are offered about virtuous moral development and learning, or practical wisdom following *phronesis*. The purpose of this section is not to offer a developed theory of virtue development or the education for *phronesis*, rather it is to offer some important points about how each have been presented in recent literature on learning virtues. The second section establishes notions of human fragility and suffering within education contexts and the work of schools. Here it is suggested that the suffering of others is perceptible to young people, and indeed forms part of their everyday lived experience through their contact with a range of sources, not least the media but also schools. The second section ends with a consideration of empathy – one of the key concepts which relates to and shapes students' engagements with human fragility and suffering in schools. Drawing on the analysis of the preceding chapters, It is argued that, so far as compassion is concerned, empathy is important but must be focused in specific ways. In particular, the sort of empathy which compassion requires of us is shaped by three conditions which bring empathy into relation with other components of compassion – recognition of fallibility, empathic distress occasioned by care for others, and *eudaimonistic* judgement. In the third section, two specific pedagogical approaches apt for exploring and cultivating these three conditions are considered, namely engaging with narratives and intersubjective communication.

Before commencing the main analysis, there is one further point which I outlined in the introduction to this book, and which I would like to repeat again here. Unlike some other works on compassion in education, my intention is not to start from a deficit model which assumes (often on the basis of conjecture rather than actual evidence) that schools, teachers, young people and communities *lack* compassion and that this is the primary reason why compassion should be taught in schools. My belief is that schools, teachers, young people and communities are already compassionate in many and varied ways (I will say a little more about this in the next chapter). For this reason, my intention in this chapter is to provide some suggestions which might provide educators with thoughts upon which they can reflect in relation to the ways schools/teachers/young people/communities are *already* compassionate, including how such compassion is framed and how it might be developed further, on the basis that there is likely to be room for all of us to be a little more compassionate in our lives, whether individually or collectively.

EDUCATING ABOUT AND FOR COMPASSION: LEARNING VIRTUE

From the outset, it is important to make clear that the analysis provided in this and the next chapter makes a number of educational assumptions. The first is that compassion is something which we can all learn, and for which we require certain educational interventions and experiences in order for it to be formed and expressed. In making this statement, I am relying on the now quite vast literature that virtues such as compassion can be taught and learned through both explicit direct teaching (in this sense, virtues can be taught) and through a range of often implicit educational processes in which general ethos and environment play a crucial role (in this sense, virtues can be caught).[1] The focus of this chapter is thus on the 'what' and the 'how' of teaching compassion, rather than 'if' it can be taught at all.

Second, and on this basis, my intention in this chapter is not to offer a fully fledged theory of young people's moral development – though it is important to say something briefly about moral development now. The positing of stages of moral development was central to Kohlberg's cognitive theory of moral learning, and has subsequently been of interest to those – like myself – who favour a virtue-centred (or character-based) approach to moral education in schools. While Aristotle himself did not provide us with a well-defined conception of moral development, a body of work has developed which has sought to either elucidate one from Aristotle's work or has sought to offer an Aristotelian informed developmental model (see Sherman 1989; Tobin 1989; Sanderse 2015; Kristjánsson 2007, 2015). In his recent, helpful work on moral development, Sanderse (2015) presents four main stages,[2] or categories derived from Aristotle's work, employing Kristjánsson's (2007, p. 20) definition of stages as 'progressive levels of moral excellence' which portray 'different developmental conditions of an agent's soul'. Sanderse highlights that unlike that Kohlberg's stages which present an 'invariant and universal sequence' with clearly separate and separated stages, the way in which individuals develop may not follow a pre-determined and ordered succession. The development of virtue, and the practical wisdom required for it, is thus a long-term and much more complex process than simple sequential models can depict. As Carr (1991, p. 9) suggests, we must be mindful that people *aspire* to possessing virtues and 'none of us can hope to afford much more than this'.

With these brief reflections in mind, and to avoid continual repetition of this point, in discussing teaching about and for compassion from an virtue-based, Aristotelian-informed perspective we must remember that children are not developing virtues through a clear and sequential process in which they master one stage before proceeding to the next. Rather, they are involved in a range complex processes through which virtue is forming and being expressed, which is not infallible, permits errors, and requires ongoing reflection and reconsideration shaped by a conception of the good life. Children (and indeed adults!) will often miss the mark of the mean, acting either in excess or deficiency of the virtue in question. Sometimes their deliberations will fall short in some way or they will lack the necessary self-control. Even if they hit the mean at one time, they may miss it in the next. In this sense, children's (and again we may add this for most adults too) virtue and practical wisdom can be understood as in development rather than as necessarily coming to full fruition in the form of the wholly compassionate (and even less, fully virtuous) person.[3] To this extent, this chapter is interested in those cultivating processes which can aid such development.

Once we turn to the specific question of how specific virtues such as compassion can be cultivated in young people, we are faced with another concern. We have seen that any Aristotelian-inspired understanding of virtues, and virtue education, places especial importance on the development of *phronesis*, or practical wisdom. Aristotle himself told us little about the educative processes as necessary for phronesis, other than his emphasis on habituation and practice. Recent scholarship on character education has started to address this gap (for an excellent overview, see Chap. 4 in Kristjánsson 2015). Julia Annas (2011) has made the case for viewing the development of *phronesis* as being similar in nature to the development of a skill. On this account, just as those who master musical or other skills do so through practice, reflection, and learning from masters, so to do those learning *phronesis*. Thus, we develop *phronesis* through our engagements – deliberate and unexpected – in practical and habitual situations and the subsequent critical reflection on such engagements which at least in part are guided by more experienced guides (such as parents and teachers). Educating for *phronesis* is therefore a planned activity, or better an ongoing set of activities) involving cognitive, affective and volitional endeavours. However, and this is crucial when we consider cultivating specific virtues such as compassion, the parallel with a skill requires something further if we are to fully understand the development of *phronesis*.

In his recent analysis of the skill analogy Kristjánsson (2015, p. 99; emphasis in original) presents a convincing case that *phronesis* requires a '*general blueprint* of the good life that can be conveyed through teaching'. To understand this argument two points are crucial. First, that unlike the acquisition of musical skills, we would want to say that the development of virtues such as compassion is important not just in relation to the contextual features of a given situation but in relation to a wider, general sense of the good life. Second, and on this basis, *phronesis* plays a role not only in guiding our response in a situation in regard to specific virtues (i.e. what is the compassionate thing to do?), but also when two or more virtues come into conflict (i.e. should I be compassionate or temperate in this situation?). As Kristjánsson (2015, p. 100) contends *phronesis* 'requires access to a systematic understanding of the good life that can *indirectly* inform and enlighten the young person's further development and decision'. As I have sought to suggest at various places throughout this book, and will try to draw out in this and the next chapter, the cultivation and expression of compassion and the practical wisdom necessary for it, cannot stand apart from wider conceptions of the good life and human flourishing.

COMPASSION, EDUCATION AND HUMAN FRAGILITY

Jeremy Waldron (2003, p. 23; emphasis added) argues that

> The moral concern we should be teaching our children is equal concern for all humans in the world; and the identity we should encourage young people to recognize is an identity that involves '*recognizing humanity* in the stranger and the other' and *responding humanely* to the human in every cultural form.

A key contention in this book has been that compassion is a particular and important way of recognising humanity and responding humanely in situations in which others are suffering, and are so in ways that have caused their humanity to be harmed, compromised and restricted. The book started by reflecting on the prevalence of suffering in the world today – suffering brought about and exacerbated by a range of factors, including conflict, disease and natural disasters. In this sense human suffering can be viewed as what Garner (2014, p. 94) terms 'an observable feature of existence'. Even if we wish to, we cannot avoid the suffering of others and must, therefore, consider how we should respond to suffering in both a general sense and in particular situations and contexts. My argument so far has been that compassion, understood as a virtue, represents a positive and morally good way of responding to suffering – one which benefits the compassionate agent, the subject of their compassion and communities more generally.

If we accept that the virtue of compassion is a worthwhile and morally valuable response to the suffering of others, a range of educational questions arise. Of these the most crucial, and one which the chapters so far have hopefully shed some light on, is how we conceive compassion and its various elements in the first place. A second question concerns those practical arrangements and processes through which compassion can be educated in young people. It is this second question which forms the main preoccupation of this and the following chapter. A third educational question so far as compassion is concerned is whether, and how, students come into relation with the suffering of others in their schools, classrooms and daily lives. This question seems both fundamental to any analysis which seeks to promote and encourage the teaching of compassion (it is difficult to suggest that schools and teachers *should* teach about and for compassion without saying at least something about what they currently *do* in this regard), yet also seems a rather difficult one to answer given that, little empirical data exists which explores directly and explicitly young people's experiences and understanding of the suffering of others. Some empirical data (which will be cited in this and the next chapter) does exist concerning teachers' understanding of compassion, but is necessarily limited in its scope (either by jurisdiction, sample size or focus). While there are a number of educational programmes which set out what education about and for compassion should/could look like (some are set out in the next chapter), there is a paucity of research on what education for and about compassion actually looks like in schools and classrooms. With this in mind, and before exploring in more detail the second question, I wish to spend a little time to say something about engaging with the suffering of others in educational contexts.

It would seem, prima facie, that the suffering of others is visible to children – not least through news and social media – on a regular and consistent basis, often through their educational experiences. Throughout their lives and experiences young people come into relation with human suffering in many ways. Some young people will have suffered or will be suffering themselves. They may see their friends and relatives suffer. They may also see suffering of different forms within the communities in which they live and engage. In addition, suffering is an almost constant feature of media broadcasts and content, and is likely to feature in discussions young people have within their homes and friendship groups. So too, in their study of curricular subjects such as English, History, Geography, Social Studies/Civics and Citizenship, and Art, and through extra-curricular activities, young people will observe and learn about a range of contexts and human interactions in which suffering is involved – whether local or global, historic or contemporary, individual or large-scale. To the extent to which we can accept that this is the case, we can say that witnessing human suffering – either directly within their communities or indirectly through the media, families and friends – forms part of the lived experience of young people today. A research I recently conducted within Australian high schools focusing on education for global citizenship suggests that, for those participants, this was certainly the case. The 13–15 year-old students with whom I spoke discussed in detail the sorts of current global issues they were hearing about through media, discussing with their families and friends, and wished they were discussing more in school. Almost always these involved the suffering of others (the European Migration Crisis, the Nepalese Earthquake, for example, were frequently cited).

If we accept, then, that suffering is an 'observable feature of existence' to return Garner's phrase, and one that is observable by young people, we must question how such observances are experienced within, mediated by, and recognised in schools and classrooms. This requires educators, of course, to think about how suffering is introduced, framed and reflected upon, as well as how awareness of the suffering of others connects to compassionate actions. Martha Nussbaum (2014, p. 204; emphasis added) advocates that '*education* in common human weakness and vulnerability should be a very profound part of the education of all children' and that 'Children should learn to be tragic spectators and to understand with subtlety and responsiveness the predicaments to which human life is prone'. Note here two crucial points. First, and similarly to Waldron's sentiments quoted above, that education for compassion necessarily brings students into relation with the suffering of others, supporting them to recognise common humanity and the fragility of the human condition. Second, that Nussbaum speaks of an *education in* common human weakness and vulnerability, not simply an exposure to it. Education for compassion is therefore an intentional act and practice which requires an engagement with and understanding of humanity, human fragility and suffering. It is an act (or better a set of acts and practices) which goes beyond superficial interactions and understandings, and which provides structured support for students to grapple with challenging thoughts, feelings and experiences.

One way in which this intentional act might take place is through the development of empathy and empathic relationships with others which recognise and respond to shared humanity. A key concern of this present book has been to suggest and explore the idea that compassion is a relational concept, and that to understand compassion we need to engage with relationality between people. It has also been suggested that central to this relationality is seeking to bring others into one's circle of concern – something which requires us to empathise with others when they are suffering. In turn, empathy requires engaging with others through various means in order that, while recognising that our imaginative reconstructions may be fallible, we can come to know something about their thoughts, feelings and goals. Within this, the inter-play between self-focused and other-focused role-taking is crucial to the development and operation of the empathy required for compassion.

The concept of empathy (often framed as an important value) is itself found much more commonly in educational policy, curricular and research discourse than is the case with compassion. Indeed, empathy has received a significant amount of positive attention in educational literature and for this reason one of the ways in which schools may currently be educating about and for compassion is likely to be through forms of empathy education. In important ways, empathy education has formed a central component of numerous educational programmes and initiatives. Not least these include the Social and Emotional Aspects of Learning (SEAL) initiative in England, the various International Baccalaureate[4] programmes, the resources offered by the Facing History and Ourselves[5] organisation, and those by the Roots of Empathy[6] program. Such programmes connect to empathy and compassion in important ways. They focus on understanding others in ways through which young people can come to recognise and appreciate humanity, including its fragility and possibilities. Often, this involves students making (inter)connections between their close and immediate associations (with peers and in their local communities, for example) and their wider, more distal, relationships. At times some rather grandiose claims have been made about the possibilities held by empathy education. One leading proponent, Roman Krznaric (2008, p. 8) claims, for example, that empathy education can bring about 'mass social change'.

Now, a minor reflection I wish to offer is that such claims must be treated with some caution, not least because (as Krznaric himself recognises) empathy education is a diverse enterprise and can (and does!) take a number of forms. If we see empathy education as both important for compassion and as vehicle through which schools can and do seek to promote notions of shared humanity, the fact that there are different forms of empathy education gives pause for thought concerning the extent to which they include three crucial conditions alluded to in previous chapters. First, that when we feel some form of empathy we must be aware that our imaginative (re)constructions are fallible and thus may be mistaken. Second, and if we remember from Chap. 3, that empathy is not in and of itself a moral enterprise, but becomes one when brought into relation with other facets of compassion – such as sympathy and care – and thus involves some form of *empathic distress*. Third, that as it connects to compassion, empathic distress is informed in important ways by our understanding of humanity *both* in terms of its fragility and the possibilities we have for flourishing. Part of the very reason we feel empathic distress when others are suffering is because we understand that their possibility for flourishing is being compromised and restricted and that this, in turn, affects our own possibilities (what, again as discussed previously, Nussbaum defines as *eudaimonistic* judgement).

When we consider examples of empathy education it is not always clear that each of these three conditions – awareness of the possibility of an empathic gap, empathic distress and *eudaimonistic* judgement – are necessarily involved. Let us consider, for example, the following vignette of a teaching episode highlighted by Krznaric (2008, p. 6) as evidencing 'empathy education in action':

> a class of eight-year-olds in Oxford studying Geography imagine what it is like to be street children in Delhi, and then write a story in the first person about the experience of leaving their village to find work in the city.

Such exercises do not seem untypical of the sorts of activities which schools and teachers seek to engage students in under the auspices of developing and expressing empathy. Krznaric (2008, p. 6; emphasis added) explains that through these activities, pupils are involved in '*comprehending* and *sharing* the emotional responses of another person'. Yet, one would want to ask some serious educational questions about what is going on here before one would want to commit to viewing the activities as developing the moral forms of empathy required for compassion. The following questions would seem to be important in this regard:

1. How have pupils engaged with others (in this case street children) in ways which avoid essentialising their conditions, contexts, lives, perspectives and goals?
2. How does the activity (or further activities) develop both other-focused role-taking and self-focused role-taking?
3. How does the imaginative reconstruction involved connect – implicitly or explicitly – to sympathy and caring for others?
4. How does the empathic response being educated connect to, and engage in reflection about, views concerning what it means to live a good life and be a good human being?

Now, it may seem unfair to pick on one example of empathy education and raise these points for my own purposes here. In response to such a criticism I can only offer the following rejoinders. First, and as mentioned above, the example does not seem to be particularly different from many others which are often cited and used in empathy education. Second, my purpose is not to criticise empathy education per se. There is much very good work which goes on under its banner, as both the *Roots of History* and *Facing History and Ourselves* demonstrate. My intention, instead, is to suggest that broad understandings of, and approaches to, empathy education are not appropriate for educating for compassion unless they pay serious attention to the three conditions stated above – (1) appreciating empathy's fallibility; (2) recognising empathy's connection with sympathy and care; and, (3) empathy's connection to conceptions of the good life and flourishing. Without doing so, the ways in which young people engage with suffering in schools would seem to be lacking in important ways. With this in mind, the next section explores the interconnections between these three conditions. In doing so, and with an awareness that there are a range of possible methods, two approaches for teaching compassion are explored – the use of narrative and intersubjective dialogue.

Empathic Fallibility, Nurturing Care and *Eudaimonistic* Judgement

It has been suggested throughout this book so far that bringing oneself into relationship with others is not easy or complete and that, as such, we must be mindful of the potential fallibility of our representations of others' viewpoints, understandings and feeling. In this section I argue that a core aim of compassionate education should be to recognise this gap and to seek to close it in appropriate and meaningful ways – ways that is which bring together empathic distress, care and considerations of the human good. In advancing this argument two particular approaches are explored: (1) the use of narratives and (2) intersubjective communication. My suggestion in focusing on these two approaches is not to deny the availability and suitability of other methods. Rather it is to argue that these two methods seem particularly appropriate, feature in current literature on character education, and serve to illustrate important considerations for teaching compassion.

Narratives: Literature and Testimonies

The use of narratives, whether in the form of literary works or personal testimonies, is a common approach for teaching character. Moreover, engaging students with narratives forms a core pedagogical strategy in a number of subject disciplines, including literature, history, social studies, art and geography. As Zagzebski (2013, p. 193) argues, 'narratives are useful for the purposes of moral education and improvement because they engage our motives much more than abstract theories, and narratives are crucial to shaping our vision of a good life'. In specific relation to literature, which will be the primary focus here, a growing body of research – often drawing on Aristotle's emphasis on the role of literature – positions students' engagement with key works as providing a fruitful approach for building the sort of imaginative reconstructions necessary for empathy and care. Martha Nussbaum (2001, p. 328) asserts the importance of literature in educating for empathy and compassion for the reason that 'only in fiction is the mind of the other transparent. The empathetic person attempts to reconstruct the mental experience of another'. Empirical evidence examining the outcomes of the Jubilee Centre for Character and Virtues' *Knightly Virtues* literacy programme reports that participation 'significantly increases pupils' ability to apply virtue language and concepts in personal contexts', and the report recommends that 'that all primary schools "teach" character education through literacy-based programmes' (Arthur et al. 2014a, p. 5).

One need not accept that fiction is the only way to engage with the minds of others in a transparent way to take the view that fiction (and I would add non-fiction to this) provides a potentially useful and valuable way of developing empathy and, for crucial our focus here, empathic distress. Literature and testimony allows us to engage with the thoughts, feelings and goals of others, tracking how these develop and respond to key experiences – what Bohlin (2005, p. 49) refers to as 'morally pivotal points' through which characters 'reassess or refine their life goal(s) or path(s)'. Through literature and testimony students can consider and explore the relationship between key elements of the characters involved and *their own* responses, while also developing an awareness of similar possibilities and an engagement in critical reflection about the good life and human flourishing. Engaging in literature can thus help children to explore and reflect on ways in which their character and actions – including virtuous actions – represent expressions of themselves. Indeed, literature seems a particularly rich resource for this enterprise and as Bohlin (2005, p. 18) contends, it can provide a tool for reflection on character which 'happens somewhere between the heart and the will, every time characters make a choice, particularly choices that somehow define who they are and mark an important change of focus'.

Of course, the selection of text and character is imperative, and it would seem of value that so far as compassion is concerned the lives of the characters are ones with which young people can engage and come to care about. In other words, that they evoke some sense of common humanity. To this end, Carr and Harrison (2015, p. 59) point to the fact that 'it is distinctive of an Aristotelian ethics of virtue and character that problems of moral life and association have very particular and distinctive human faces'. Focusing specifically on literature and the education of compassion, my intention here is not to detail a lengthy list of texts and characters suitable for this purpose; this would be better done by those with a wider and deeper literary knowledge than my own, though perhaps it should be noted that across the literature there is a preference for focuses on texts with sufficient depth[7] (see, e.g., Nussbaum 2001; Bohlin 2005).[8] Nor is my intention to provide the full multitude of possibilities held by literature for educators seeking to engage students in compassion (Bohlin's (2005) text provides the best exploration currently available). My intention instead is to suggest that literature provides two particular frames for fostering empathy, empathic distress and engaging students with compassion.

One frame is to study characters who themselves might be said to exhibit compassion. While it may be possible to find characters who are characteristically good (such as Little Nell, Lucie Manette or Atticus Finch), it is more likely – and perhaps more valuable – for young people to study literary figures whose compassion forms part of (or indeed changes) a more complex character and whose 'compassion' is open to discussion and interpretation (such as whether key responses and actions by, for example, Sydney Carlton in Dickens' *A Tale of Two Cities* or the whisky priest in Greene's *The Power and the Glory* can be considered compassionate). As Bohlin (2005, p. 25) persuasively argues, 'our goal is not to learn so much by imitation as by ethical reflection. Our goal is to learn from their mistakes as well as their successes, and to evaluate the merits and limitations of their desired destinations'. Bohlin sets out four common features – each of them apt for exploring compassion – upon which teachers can focus in teaching character through literature: (1) 'relationships', (2) 'learning from pain and acquiring new pleasures', (3) 'thoughtful reflection' and (4) 'courage to face the truth (about reality, oneself and others)' (2005, p. 25). Through these features, students can be encouraged and supported to think about (and indeed feel) the moral perspectives, characteristics and actions of the protagonists involved –

including their intended, and at times revised, conceptions of the good and the factors which influence them.

This view, which is one I take others such as Carr and Harrison as well as Bohlin to subscribe to, understands narratives to be valuable because they provide an insight into and a vehicle for exploring not just what a good person is, but what it means to be a good person in the first place and what it is that makes people good. This is a notably different tact to that advocated by Zagzebski (2013) who in her moral "theory" based on moral exemplars proposes the notion that what is required from moral theory, and what moral exemplars provide, is an available and meaningful depiction or representation of what it without necessarily employing the associated descriptive concepts following means to be good. According to Zagzebski (2013, p. 199; emphasis in original),

> good persons are persons *like that*, just as gold is stuff *like that*. Picking out exemplars can fix the reference of the term 'good person' without the use of descriptive concepts. It is not necessary for ordinary people engaged in moral practice to know the nature of good persons – what makes them good. In fact, it is not necessary that anybody knows what makes a good person good in order to successfully refer to good persons.

Zagzebski's position is hard to accept given that it neglects the importance of exploring, knowing and appreciate fully what being good is – including developing the moral vocabulary necessary for such tasks. Without an available conception of the good it is not clear how thoughts, emotions and actions which constitute the good can be identified, appraised and desired accordingly. When we consider good persons as being *like that* we do so because they bear some relation to our wider notion of what a good person actually is and because we are (or at least should be) making some form of evaluative judgement about what it is that makes them good, deploying concepts as we do so. While there may be different reasons for our accounts of what makes people good, there are reasons nevertheless and ones which need to be included in any meaningful exploration of moral life.

A second frame for exploring compassion in literature is to support students' development and critical inquiry in specific relation to the characters in the text. In this way, rather than considering whether a given protagonist is compassionate, students explore whether they themselves do or should feel compassion for the given literary character. Here the focus changes from, for example, in what ways might Sydney Carlton be considered compassionate, to whether we do or should feel compassion for Sydney Carlton and for what reasons. Similarly to the first frame, this second approach can allow and enable students to build relationships with the characters in the text, invoking students' empathy and concern while also requiring them to explore morally salient features of characters, contexts and experiences (such learning would seem to be a central focus when teaching books such as *The Boy in the Striped Pyjamas* or engaging with films such as *Rabbit-Proof Fence* – or indeed in engaging in personal testimonies about people's experiences and understandings of particular situations, events and relationships).

This second approach to framing also opens up the possibility for students to engage in notions of deservingness in relation to compassion. In Chap. 2 it was discussed that for some commentators (most notably Aristotle, and Nussbaum's Aristotelian-informed contemporary account) an important condition of compassion is the extent to which the suffering caused can be said to be undeserved. On such accounts deservingness manifests in two ways. First, that the suffering is the result of no culpability of those suffering, and second, that those suffering are culpable to an extent but the degree of suffering can be said to be disproportionate to the degree of culpability. An argument was also made that notions of desert are problematic so far as compassion is concerned, and that the moral agent can feel compassion for those who are in some way culpable for their suffering, making use of practical wisdom in doing so.

Engaging students with narratives – either though literature or testimonies – provides potential to examine notions of deservingness, culpability and compassion in ways which explore the causes of suffering, the question of culpability and the ways in which these shape and effect the empathic distress and care for others. The tragedies of Shakespeare, and in particular *Macbeth* and *Coriolanus*, provide complex and highly nuanced accounts of the human condition through which compassion, empathy and care can be explored. Indeed, whether we can (or even should) feel some sort of care or compassion for Macbeth, for example, despite his actions appears to be a central question in any exploration of that particular text and brings into attention his psychology, his culpability, his relationships, and his humanity. As such, through focusing on the suffering of those who may be understood as in some way culpable for the suffering they experience, the scope of compassion is extended. To express compassion in this way requires a great deal of the compassionate agent, not least in the form of discerning action (or perhaps even inaction) that is appropriate and may, where personal testimonies are involved in particular, take us to some quite difficult places which will not always be appropriate for the classroom (teachers are the best judges of treading this line in sensitive and appropriate ways, of course). We should remember, though, that if students are taught only to be compassionate to those who are undeserving of their suffering we are – either explicitly or implicitly – asking them to narrow their circle of concern, limiting or denying the humanity they see in others.

Intersubjective Communication

If we are to seek to understand the other – their emotions, their thoughts, their goals – intersubjective communication would seem to be of central importance. Understood broadly as the free and open exchange of ideas through a range of verbal and non-verbal methods, intersubjective communication is integral to the development of empathy, and provides a crucial mechanism for the 'sharing of affective states' (Schertz 2007, p. 186). As such, it is through intersubjective communication that empathy can not only develop, but can do so in ways which support the closing of empathic gaps as ideas, meaning and arguments are shared, explored and refined. Where possible, intersubjective communication requires a range of capacities, particularly where compassionate relationships are concerned. These include trust, humility, open-mindedness, honesty and kindness, to name a few. Of course, direct dialogue with others is not always possible or appropriate in the classroom, and so schools and teachers need to rely on a range of techniques and strategies for developing intersubjective communication. Within these personal testimonies/histories and other forms of narratives will be a crucial part, and will be supplemented by a range of visual media (for an argument in favour of the use of testimonies see, e.g., Boler 1999).

Intersubjective communication, then, represents a crucial process through which children can *recognise* others. Indeed, recognition (or misrecognition when a gap exists) can be viewed as a crucial component of closing the empathic gap. When we come into relation with those suffering in ways which fail to respond to their humanity, or which deny them their own sense of empowerment and human flourishing, recognition is at best limited, and at worst denied. Recognition on this account forms a fundamental basis of social justice (see Fraser (2005) for example), meaning that education for and about compassion education which does not engage seriously with the actual perspectives of those suffering, or does so from a particular gaze or in a superficial way, runs the risk of misrecognition. As Charles Taylor (1992, pp. 25–26; emphasis in original) suggests,

> Our identity is partly shaped by recognition or its absence, often by the *mis*recognition of others, and so a person or group of people can suffer real damage, real distortion, if the people of a society around them mirror back a confining or demeaning or contemptible picture of themselves. Non recognition or misrecognition can inflict harm, can be a form of oppression, imprisoning some in a false, distorted, and reduced mode of being.

While Taylor's remarks concern recognition generally, they are no less important so far as compassion is concerned. Indeed, and to repeat, forms of compassion resting on the *mis*recognition of others would be compromised in some way. Developing communication, such as through dialogical interactions, *between children in classrooms* also seems crucial in developing empathy and seeking to close empathic gaps. When children discuss and reflect on their understanding of others and when they share their self- and other-focused role-taking perspectives, different interpretations become shared and are able to be analysed in critical ways.

For educators wishing to cultivate compassion, it is necessary, therefore, that thought is given to the ways in which teaching, learning and the curriculum recognises – or indeed fails to recognise – the particular perspectives and circumstances of those suffering. Without attending to these, important agent (both the compassionate subject and object) and situation specific factors will remain obscured or missed altogether and compassionate intent runs the risk of missing the mark. The focus on recognition and the necessity of intersubjective communication thus raises important questions for schools and teachers about the extent to which, and the ways in which, students can be supported to engage in varied forms of deliberation and discussion in order to understand and engage with the sentiments and goals of others and to bring these into relation with their own. In turn, this also involves considering how understanding and engaging with the sentiments of others can be aided by others in close proximity, for example peers or teachers.

As part of this endeavour, students are involved in articulating their interests, and coming to know the interests of others, through dialogical processes. Further, through discussing their interpretations and understandings of others with others (peers, teachers) these can be offered up for further scrutiny and revision. To this end, the various capacities central to compassion – including empathic distress, care, *eudaimonistic* judgement – can become regulatory principles within the classroom which promote intellectual humility and open-mindedness. This intention is central to the following remarks from the Swedish National Agency for Education (2000, p. 8) which present a clear elucidation of the goals of dialogical interaction in the classroom: 'dialogue allows differing views and values to confront one another and develop. Dialogue allows individuals to make their own ethical judgements by listening, reflecting, finding arguments and appraising, while it also constitutes an important point of developing an understanding of one's own views and those of others'. As Benjamin Barber (2003, p. 175) reflects, through such communication 'I will put myself in his place. I will try to understand. I will strain to hear what makes us alike, I will listen for a common rhetoric evocative of a common purpose or a common good'.

Through recognising others and sharing interests in a dialogical way, it is likely that the care for others will also be an important outcome. As we saw in the third chapter, the relationship between empathic distress and the principle of care is an important one so far as compassion is concerned. Care moves our empathy from recognising that there is another who is suffering to being distressed at that suffering and, as a result, caring enough for the other to *actively help*. The connection between *dialogue* and care is central to this process, and its education. As Noddings (2005, p. 23) suggests,

> Dialogue...connects us to each other and helps to maintain caring relations. It also provides us with the knowledge of each other that forms a foundation for response in caring...We respond most effectively as carers when we understand what the other needs and the history of this need. To receive the other is to attend fully and openly. Continuing dialogue builds up a substantial knowledge of one another that serves to guide our responses.

As part of their *Making Caring Common Project*, the Harvard Graduate School of Education (2014, p. 15) explain this process as one in which students 'zoom in' with their peers in ways which then enable them to 'zoom out' to consider the perspectives of, and to expend their care to, others:

> Children and youth need to learn to zoom in, listening closely and attending to those in their immediate circle, and to zoom out, taking in the big picture and

considering multiple perspectives. It is by zooming out and taking multiple perspectives, including the perspectives of those who are too often invisible (such as the new kid in class, someone who doesn't speak their language, or the school custodian), that young people expand their circle of concern and become able to consider the justice of their communities and society.

Care also plays a role in seeking to ensure that the empathy developed through intersubjective communication is sincere. That empathy may not be sincere is a particular concern for cultivating compassion. The concern here is that while young people may present an empathic response, this may lack sincerity (in the words of George Burns, 'sincerity – if you can fake that, you've got it made'). Clearly, there are no easy answers to this question. Some children may see forms of intersubjective communication largely as an academic exercise within which they present the sorts of responses they think are likely to be welcomed or which enable them to attain good grades. This lack of authenticity may then lead to a lack of transferal to other contexts. When care is involved, however, the chances that intersubjective communication will lack authenticity is likely to be diminished. Our responses are informed by our relationship with others in a way which goes beyond seeing them as simply an interlocutor there for the benefits of our own ends or to be out-argued, but as another human being with whom we are participating in a shared enterprise.

If we accept that dialogical intersubjective communication is an important way in which empathy and care can be developed, it remains for us to consider the form and intention that such dialogue should take in more detail. Work in the field of civic and citizenship education reminds us that communication and deliberation can adopt two main purposes within classrooms (Parker 2003, 2006; Hess 2009; Peterson 2009; Peterson and Warwick 2014). Hess (2009, p. 85; emphasis in original) reminds us that educators may aim at 'teaching *for* and *with* discussion' and that communication 'is both a desired outcome and a method of teaching', whilst Parker (2006, p. 12), on whom Hess draws, remarks that the 'two kinds of discourse are complimentary in school practice, and neither is sufficient alone'. For Parker, discussion aims at both 'enriching the mind and cultivating a democratic political community' – a political community which so far as compassion is concerned can be understood as incorporating those beyond one's national borders.

Of course, how communication is structured and enacted plays a crucial role in its effectiveness and operation, something which is particularly apt for cultivating compassion. This requires us to consider carefully how dialogue with others outside of and within classrooms and schools is approached. While the conflict of ideas and the generation of emotional responses are not in and of themselves problematic, they become so when priority is placed on point-scoring, bettering others and 'winning the debate'. Under such conditions, the sorts of care, reflection and interchange central for learning about and for compassion are likely to become compromised. It seems beneficial, therefore, that central to communication is the acceptance that it is a collaborative, co-operative and shared endeavour rather than one which is competitive and individualised. To this end, the following reflection from Elizabeth McGrath (cited in Nash 1997, p. 147) seems apt:

> Many people seem compelled to jump into a heated argument the moment they have sense a different opinion...This tendency may be natural, but it need not be controlling. We can learn to acknowledge, without feeling threatened, the value of ideas that do not fit our system...[when I acknowledge the other] I am simply offering to that person the dignity, support, and encouragement that I myself need as I inch my way along the path. In short, we can choose to act as effective catalysts and staunch supports for one another or we can make [dialogue] even more difficult and painful by fuelling the fires of self-doubt in ourselves and others.

Approached in this way, intersubjective communication includes a commitment not only to observing and speaking, but also to listening to others. As Barber (1998, p. 118) suggests, we must remember that we 'not only ha[ve] a voice, but an ear' and that the skills of listening are 'as important as the skills of talking...talk as communication...involves receiving as well as expressing, hearing as well as speaking, and emphasizing as well as uttering' (2003, p. 174). Hearing the perspectives of those suffering represents, then, not only an essential element of compassion but of educating about and for compassion.

For compassion, listening to others in this way necessarily includes, but moves beyond, immediate experiences and considerations. While these are central, as we have seen, compassion in part represents an expression of the sort of person we are and wish to be. Moreover, when we respond to the suffering of others with compassion a *eudaimonistic* judgement is involved through which the flourishing of the other, and the restrictions placed on flourishing by the causes of suffering, becomes part of our own conception of flourishing. As Nussbaum (2001, p. 432) suggests, an education for compassionate citizenship should also be a multicultural education. Our pupils must learn to appreciate the diversity of circumstances in which human beings struggle for flourishing; this means not just learning some facts about classes, races, nationalities, sexual orientations other than her own, but being drawn into those lives, through the imagination, becoming a participant in those struggles.

The listening involved in compassionate exchange involves students, then, in engagements about the good life and notions of flourishing held by both the other and themselves.

Moreover, in order to engage with notions of the good life with others, it seems necessary that students are able to listen to their own thoughts, feelings and conceptions. Engaging with others in the form needed for compassion requires, that is, a degree of reflexivity. As Benhabib (1996, pp. 71–72) has argued,

> the very procedure of articulating a view in public imposes a certain reflexivity on individual preferences and opinions... The process of articulating good reasons in public forces the individual to think of what would count as a good reasons for all others involved.

Goodin (2003a, 2003b) refers to this process as involving 'internal-reflection', and understands this as involving the cognitive and emotional faculties within us which are necessarily stimulated through dialogical interaction with others. The reflexivity involved in, and necessary for, intersubjective communication is likely to take place at various stages of dialogical interaction and is crucial to the sort of critical reflection central to the development of practical wisdom. This connection is illustrated in relation to habituation – a core process through which learning the virtues takes places. While a narrow understanding of habituation would read it as referring simply to practice, a wider and more developed notion understands that habituation requires critical reflection and reflexivity in order to be effective (and in this sense is an appropriate focus for intersubjective communication).

Recent research evidence on educational dialogue concerning notions of the good life, however, paints a somewhat mixed picture of students' reflexivity. In his research on education for global citizenship, Dill (2013, p. 96) reports that across participant schools in the USA, 'the universal global citizen seems to take a highly particularized form', one which 'reflects a Western, liberal, rational, secular and consumerist account'. Here Dill draws on the work of John Boli (2005) to suggest that there is a kind of 'façade diversity'. For Dill, this façade serves to 'homogenize to a vision of the individual stripped of collective identities', resulting in a projection of dominant commitments onto others. In other words, students see others through their own, frequently uncritical, lens in ways which fail to appreciate the full picture or which serve to promote particular or idealised interests without fully engaging with the other. For the students in Dill's research it seems that their own accounts of flourishing are positioned on to others, rather than truly coming into relation with others. Yet, evidence from the extensive Religion in Education: A contribution to Dialogue or a factor of Conflict in transforming societies of European countries (REDco) project suggests not only that 'students wish for peaceful coexistence across difference and believe this to be possible', but also that students view this as dependent on 'knowledge about each other's religions and worldviews' (Jackson 2009, p. 35). For these students, knowledge about others' conceptions of the good seems to be viewed as valuable and important for human relationships with others. Indeed, an important finding deriving from the REDco project is the need for, and value of, students engaging with worldviews in order to develop reflexivity alongside edification (understanding and reflecting on how engagement with the ideas and beliefs of others stands in relation to their own conceptions and understandings; see Jackson 2009, 2012).

CONCLUSION

In this chapter I have sought to advance and defend the view that education about and for compassion must start from an awareness that human suffering and fragility are features of young people's everyday lived experiences in the sense, at least, that images of suffering are conveyed to them through various mediums, including schools themselves. From this perspective the educational question of import is not whether young people should engage with compassion and its inter-related components, but how compassion is engaged and could be engaged with more. In addition, a further question of importance is how teaching can respond in supportive and educative ways. Central to understanding meaningful responses to both of these questions is how compassion and its components are framed within educational curricular and pedagogies. Drawing on the core principle of empathy to illustrate this point, it has been argued that approaches to teaching empathy for those who are suffering come closer to compassion when they are framed by three particular conditions – recognition of empathic fallibility, empathic distress occasioned by care for others, and *eudaimonistic* judgement. Though two pedagogical approaches which seem particularly conducive to cultivating compassion have been explored, conditions such as these which develop from understanding compassion as a virtue provide a valuable and morally relevant frame for conceiving and positioning other pedagogical responses. Moreover, they are also relevant to a view of learning virtue which accepts that to be fully virtuous (either generally or with regards to a specific virtue) is something of an ideal, and that moral development is a guided process involving trial, error, reflection and subsequent adaptation in the pursuit of practical wisdom.

Notes

1. A range of studies provides empirical data to 'support the view that the capacity for empathy or sympathy . . . continues to increase with age from the early years into adolescence' (Eisenberg et al. 2006, p. 521; see also Hoffman 2000). Emerging findings in the field of psychology and neuroscience with young adults also supports the notion that compassion can be learned. See, for example, Weng et al. (2013).
2. These are 'moral indifference', 'lack of self-control', 'self-control' and 'proper virtue'.
3. On this point Sanderse (2015, p. 393) indicates his 'doubt whether Aristotle's ideal [proper virtue] . . . can ever be exemplified by anyone . . . Instead, we can think of the "last" stage of moral development as an intermediate and open-ended level: even for the virtuous person there is room for improvement'.
4. In its learner profile, the International Baccalaureate includes empathy within 'caring' which is defined as 'we show empathy, compassion and respect. We have a commitment to service, and we act to make a positive difference in the lives of others and in the world around us' (IB 2013, p. 5).
5. https://www.facinghistory.org/
6. http://www.rootsofempathy.org/
7. According to Nussbaum (2001, p. 433) 'the fact that Sophoclean tragedy inspires compassion for human suffering and the fact that it is great and powerful poetry are not independent facts: it is the poetic excellence that convey compassion to the spectator, cutting through the habits of the everyday', while Bohlin (2005, p. 15) identifies the challenges educators face from 'the range of negative narrative images and stimuli that feed the

imaginations and aspirations of young people', including 'widely popularized books that idealize the fast track to fame and fortune'.

8. Noakes (2014) cites a range of possible texts for exploring compassion in English literature classrooms, including Shakespeare's *Othello*, Susan Hill's *I'm the King of the Castle* and Stephen King's *The Body*.

CHAPTER 7

Schools as Compassionate Institutions: Teachers, Families and Communities

INTRODUCTION

While compassion primarily takes the form of an individual response to the suffering of others, it does not operate within a vacuum. As we have seen in various ways throughout this book, compassion is shaped, disrupted and informed by institutional processes and structures. That this is so requires us to consider the extent to which schools – and the teachers who work within them – promote or inhibit compassion through their general ethos, culture and practices. As the *Framework for Character Education* published by the Jubilee Centre for Character and Virtues at the University of Birmingham suggests, 'character is largely caught through role-modelling and emotional contagion. School culture and ethos are therefore essential.' In turn this also prompts consideration of the ways in which schools relate to the families of their students as well as to the wider communities in which they (both schools and families) are situated.

With this in mind, this chapter offers an exploration of what it might mean for schools to be compassionate institutions. It should be noted from the outset that the arguments offered here are somewhat tentative, given that while the notion of compassionate institutions is one which is often advocated, what this actually means in practice is not always immediately clear. Moreover, it is also important to state that, as with individuals, the question of whether schools are compassionate institutions or not is one which defies a precise answer. As with individuals, schools are

© The Author(s) 2017
A. Peterson, *Compassion and Education*,
DOI 10.1057/978-1-137-54838-2_7

likely to be compassionate in some ways, and uncompassionate in others; compassionate at some times and uncompassionate at others. If we accept that this is, at least prima facie, likely to be the case our focus becomes concerned not with whether schools are or are not compassionate, but how they are already compassionate and how this compassion might be developed further in appropriate ways.

The need for a balanced approach can be illustrated though reference to the fact that a number of recent calls for compassionate schooling employ idealistic rhetoric. Coles (2015a, p. 22), for example, posits the following ambitious intention for education:

> The end is clear. We must produce a global compassionate education service, must change the story so that future generations inherit a world based on love with collaboration and service at its core.

While such claims provide vision and are certainly well intentioned, there is a possibility that they can become detached (intentionally or unintentionally) from the reality of schools' moral work. Though little empirical research exists which focuses specifically on compassion in schools, some research evidence available from the UK concerning moral climate more generally highlights that while there may well be scope for further development, there is an *existing* foundation of moral cultivation and practice in schools. In their study *Character Education in UK Schools*, Arthur et al. (2015a, p. 5) found that over half of participating secondary school teachers and four-fifths of primary school teachers reported that 'their school already had a "whole school approach to character building"', while '59 % of primary school teachers believed that their school placed a "very high" priority on moral teaching'. With this in mind, while in this chapter I offer some suggestions for cultivating compassion within whole-school contexts in partnership with families and communities, these are likely to be of far less value if they do not coalesce with, and build on, existing practices which serve to develop compassion.

This final chapter is structured around two sections. In the first, the work of teachers and schools in educating about and for compassion are explored. Unlike the previous chapter which focused on the curriculum and pedagogy, the attention here is afforded to wider processes central to schooling and teaching. Examining what it might mean to be for schools to be and become compassionate institutions. It is argued that wider school processes and the general work of teachers both play a core part of cultivating compassion, but that within these moral vocabulary relating to compassion needs to be explicit. Important in this regard are the ways that teachers understand their role as moral educators and in turn position and frame certain educative connections and activities. In the second section, focus moves to the relationships schools and teachers have with families and communities as they relate to compassion. In this section some possible tensions which make possible a mismatch between intention and practice in this regard are considered. In light of these it is suggested that partnerships built on mutuality, partnership and reciprocity are likely to be more effective in developing compassion than those built on distrust and deficit. In the conclusion some thoughts are also given about teacher preparation.

Teachers and Schools

Schools

The Jubilee Centre for Character and Virtues' *Framework for Character Education* (2013; emphasis added) makes clear that

> Belonging to a school community is a deeply formative experience that helps make students the kind of persons they become. In a wide sense, character education permeates all subjects, wider school activities and general school ethos; it cultivates the virtues of character associated with common morality and develops students' understanding of what is excellent in diverse spheres of human endeavour. Schools do and should aid students in knowing the good, loving the good and doing the good. Schools should enable students to become good persons and citizens, able to lead good lives, as well as 'successful' persons. Schooling is concerned centrally with the formation of character and benefits from an *intentional and planned approach* to character development.

Central here, as emphasised, is that schools' approaches to character education should not be left implicit or to chance, but rather should be intentional and planned. That is, it is important that educators reflect on and actively plan the ways in which various facets of schooling, including ethos, culture, teacher relationships, and community and family connections, serve or detract from the education of character. This recognition is relevant both to the education of character generally and to the cultivation of compassion, and thus prompts us to reflect on the ways in which schools are 'compassionate institutions'. For the purpose of this chapter, I conceive the term compassionate institution broadly and understand it to refer to an institution which values compassion, uses a vocabulary of compassion, and which seeks to develop and promote relationships based on care, empathy, altruism and a positive form of self-love.

While we may accept this general definition of a compassionate institution, typically, as will be explored in this section, definitions of compassionate schools consist of aspirational statements or commitments rather than empirically evaluated practices. Before examining some recent examples of such statements, I would like to briefly consider an interesting study provided by Lilius et al. (2011, p. 874), who use the term 'compassion capability' to refer to 'the reliable capacity of members of a collective to notice, feel and respond to suffering'. In their research of a business organisation in the USA, Lilius et al. found two relational conditions to be central in fostering members to notice, feel and respond to the suffering of colleagues. While developed in a business setting, these conditions are likely to be of interest to schools.

The first relational condition is described by Lilius et al. (2011, p. 886) as being 'high-quality connections', or in other words the extent to which they held each other in high positive regard. This condition was seen to be engendered by a range of relational practices and processes through which colleagues within the organisation felt valued themselves as well as valuing others. Such activities included being involved in collective decision-making processes, systems through which colleagues are recognised, acknowledged and celebrated, and procedures for handling and rectifying conflict. For Lilius et al. high-quality connections serve to develop compassionate capability through increasing (1) the extent to which colleagues are attuned to each other, (2) identification with the group as a meaningful and mutually productive collectivity within which empathy and empathic concern play a vital role, and (3) permitting and facilitating continuous dialogue between colleagues about their respective positions, including their need for and ability to provide help and support.

The second relational condition is described by Lilius et al. (2011, p. 886) as being 'a dynamic boundary-permeability norm', or in other words flexibility on behalf of respondents to blur clear distinctions between their work and non-work lives. This is seen to be particularly important in permitting respondents to view each other as *both* colleague and human, rather than just the former. Of course, this did not mean that the distinction was blurred fully or constantly – there are times where to do so would be inappropriate and unproductive – hence the use of the adjective *dynamic*. For these respondents there was an important interplay and reimagining at different times of these categories. Lilius et al. cite a range of practices as particularly important in shaping this dynamic boundary-permeability norm, including celebrating significant events in colleagues' private lives, social events and accepted 'bounded playing', and addressing conflict. For Lilius et al. a dynamic boundary-permeability norm serves to develop compassionate capability (1) through increasing the sharing of information – including pertinent non-work information – between colleagues, and, as a result of this sharing of information, (2) a knowledge and understanding of others who may have been in similar situations and who may be 'a particular source of insight or comfort' (2011, p. 890). Such thoughts provide a potentially useful frame for schools to consider their own practices in relation to compassion.

As suggested above, however, most accounts of schools as compassionate institutions depend largely on aspirational statements of commitments. The Charter for Compassion[1] organisation, for example, offers the following charter for compassionate schools:

We...declare our shared commitment to the following principles, and pledge to hold ourselves and one another accountable to their realization.

We recognize that every person shares a common humanity capable both of happiness and suffering. We pledge in our words and actions to treat everyone in this school community as we would wish to be treated, to help those around us who are in need, and to make amends when we cause another pain.

We recognize that we are a school with different abilities, body sizes, races, religions, classes, gender identities and sexual orientations. We pledge to step into the shoes of others and see how things look from their point of view, especially when we disagree or find ourselves in conflict.

We recognize that intolerance and hatred cause suffering and that when we stand by doing nothing, or laugh or post comments online when others bully, we contribute to the problem. We pledge to stand up to bullying and make this a school where everyone belongs.

In signing, we commit to practice the values in this Charter within our school community; in our daily interactions, whether teacher-to-teacher, teacher-to-student, or student-to-student; and in the projects we undertake within our community and in the world.

Coles (2015a) cites the work of Pam Cayton, Headteacher of the Tara Redwood School in California and developer of the *Creating Compassionate Cultures* programme, as providing a useful illustration of how schools can develop a compassionate culture. The programme[2] posits 'seven steps to knowledge, strength and compassion', through which schools can teach and build compassion. The steps are 'mindful intention' (understanding what we want and what makes us happy), 'interconnection' (the interconnectedness of the world), 'change' (recognising the existence of change and the possibilities change offers), 'perception' (creating a view of ourselves and the world), 'transformation' (experiencing emotions and negative events in a positive way), 'empathy' ('extending understanding to others') and 'compassion' (beneficial actions 'towards others and ourselves'). Approaches such as *Creating Compassionate Cultures* provide what might be termed a 'composite' approach to developing compassionate institutions in which cultivating compassion is not reducible to a single (or even a few) practices, but rather involves a range practices, values and commitments which work together towards compassion. We notice, for example, that only the seventh step mentions compassion explicitly. We can see this too in the Guidelines for Teachers, Cayton (2011, p. 14; cited in Cole 2015a, p. 21) sets out a number of qualities of the compassionate teacher: 'the teacher as a firm but loving guide'; 'the teacher who hears the children's point of view', and the teacher who can 'enjoy life as it comes: be serious about humour and plan for spontaneity'.

This composite approach is also evident in John Lloyd's (2015) exploration of education for compassion through health and well-being, in which he reworks the ten principles of effective personal, social and health education provided by the PSHE[3] association in England with compassion in mind. Compassionate schools are positioned as incorporating the following principles within their curriculum (note that the plain text is taken from the original principles, and the italicised text are Lloyd's representations of how a compassionate school would respond):

1. Start where children and young people are: *ask them, respond appropriately to their questions, use draw and write..., focus groups, questionnaires and make use of locally available data;*
2. Plan a 'spiral programme' which introduces new and more challenging learning: *not repetitive but developmental, showing progression;*

3. Take a positive approach which does not attempt to induce shock or guilt: *this deals with and manages risk and challenge and develops resilience*;
4. Offer a wide variety of teaching and learning styles: *this recognizes the benefits of class teaching, work in small groups, individual work as well as role play, simulations, drama*;
5. Provide information that is realistic and relevant: *use data about young peoples' behaviour that challenges and provides a normative approach*;
6. Encourage young people to reflect on their learning: *this offers self-reflection and regular assessment of work, shows progress; in secondary schools, offer accreditation through ASDAN, OCR and AQA*[4];
7. Recognize that the PSHE programme is just one part of what a school can do: *this offers opportunities for personal development across and beyond the school curriculum, character-building activities, opportunities to participate*;
8. Embed PSHE within other efforts: *this recognizes the opportunity for effective PSHE through cross-curricular approaches*;
9. Provide opportunities for children and young people to make real decisions: *this recognizes the influences – their friends, the media, and social networks – on their decision-making*;
10. Provide a safe and supportive learning environment: *this deals with misbehaviour, harassment and bullying* (Lloyd 2015, p. 103–104).

The qualities identified by Lloyd here point to what we might expect of compassionate schools and teachers, but one could equally say that these qualities are ones which designate the loving and kind teacher. In other words, we may ask: what is it about these qualities which make them precisely and specifically compassionate?

I think there are two responses to this question which require some elucidation – one which broadly is supportive of the approaches taken above and one which seeks to add something further. To start with the first response, composite approaches which view compassion – and compassionate education – as involving a range of factors, qualities and capacities offer more potential for educators than approaches which seek to reduce compassion to a catch-all sentence. The lists above, and others are available (see, Coles (2015b) for example), all point to a range of conceptual and practical foci which can aid schools in the teaching and cultivation of compassion. Such an approach is appropriate given the complexity of com-passion, and its focus on a range of capacities required for its development. As the proceeding chapters made clear, these capacities – each necessary, none sufficient alone – include recognition of suffering, a concern for humanity, an appreciation of human fragility, empathic distress, the principle of care and compassionate action.

Spelling out these capacities again here, though, serves to highlight a second response which needs to be considered and included in any composite approaches to compassionate schooling. This is the need to ensure that such approaches are specifically and *explicitly* moral in their outlook, and relate to notions of common humanity and care for others (as we see in the Charter for Compassionate Schools) *and* to ideas of the good life and human flourishing (which at best is implicitly alluded to in the approaches above). Without this latter connection – without that is an appreciation that compassion and suffer-ing involve judgements about what it means to be human, what it means for humans to live a good life, and what constitutes human flourishing – some-thing essential to and for compassion is underplayed, or neglected altogether.

Teachers

To a large extent, and in important ways, whether connections are made to morality and conceptions of the good will be dependent on how teachers view themselves as moral educators and how they understand the nature of teachers' work. In his seminal text on educating the virtues, David Carr (1991, p. 10) concluded that 'a good moral educator can only be one who himself aspires to the achievement of some degree of moral excellence characterisable in terms of such attitudes and dispositions as honesty, courage, self-control, integrity, benevolence and so forth'. Recent research published by the Jubilee Centre for Character and Virtues presents a mixed picture of teachers' views and work in cultivating character. The research reports that the teachers in the study 'saw character education as integral to their teaching', 'confirmed...that they frequently draw upon virtue-based reasoning in the classroom, especially in areas of moral or practical significance', and also found that 'a large number of teachers also had high expectations of the difference they can make with the children they teach' (Arthur et al. 2015b, p. 5). The research also found, however, that a range of factors placed restrictions on teachers' moral work (a point to which we return in more detail below).

Here I would like to consider further two practically concerned ways in which how teachers understand themselves and their role as moral educators impacts on the educational experiences of their students – (1) role-modelling and (2) student action – both of which are crucial for cultivating compassion character within schools.

Role-modelling – or the use of moral examples/exemplars – is a core strategy within the toolkit of character educators, and requires that teachers think about their own character and conduct (teachers-as-role-models) as well as the figures they draw on (others-as-role-models) in cultivating virtue (given that I have considered others-as-role-models in relation to narratives in the previous chapter, my focus here will be on teachers-as-role-models). So far as teachers-as-role-models is concerned, most advocates of character education view this to be a crucial pedagogical approach,[5] with young people learning through a varied process of observing, reflecting and seeking to emulate[6] the virtues being modelled. For Lickona (2004, p. 118), teachers' own characters are 'the most important moral lesson in the character curriculum'. Yet, research suggests that while teachers view their role-modelling responsibilities as an important part of their work, they often find it difficult to conceive and enact in practice (Kristjánsson 2015). In addition, Sanderse (2013) points to the fact that not all teachers will be virtuous, and that some teachers might be 'weak, spiteful, vain and greedy, thereby qualifying as bad teachers'. Reviewing empirical data, Sanderse also suggests that much role-modelling remains implicit, and that students often place low importance on teachers as role models (as opposed to relatives, for example).

To cultivate compassion, then, some thought needs to be given as to the ways in which teachers act as compassionate role models. It is necessary to note here that recent empirical evidence on how teachers understand themselves as role-models for compassion is rather limited, and much of what does exist focuses on strands of compassion, such as care, or adjuncts of compassion, such as mindfulness. One recent study of teacher character strengths reveals that fairness (55 %) and kindness (49 %) were within the top six characteristics teachers reported they possessed, but unlike fairness (over 80 %), kindness was not viewed as being in the top six character strengths of the 'ideal' teacher in which perseverance and leadership were preferred (Arthur et al. 2015a).

That these respondents did not place kindness (the closest attribute to compassion or caring on the scale employed[7]) within the top six characteristics of an ideal teacher is not insignificant. From a care-ethics perspective, Noddings (2012, p. 772) cites the importance of teachers acting as caring role-models, asking the question 'when should teachers put aside the assumed need to learn a specific aspect of subject matter and address the expressed need of the student for emotional support, moral direction, or shared human interest?'. Central to Noddings' response is her contentions, first, that caring focuses on the relation between the carer and the cared-for, and second, that caring relations involve four core stages: (1) the carer is attentive, (2) the carer attends, (3) the carer responds and (4) the cared-for responds to 'show that the caring has been received'. For teachers, according to Noddings, the aim – attained through these stages – should be to ensure that their caring responses to students are based on 'expressed needs' (what the child actually wants) rather than 'assumed needs' (what the teacher thinks the child should want).

In making this claim, Noddings draws a distinction which is of relevance to our discussion here, one which is problematic but serves to clarify my own position. After positioning caring as relation, Noddings (2012, p. 773; emphasis original; see also Noddings 2001) argues that

> There is, however, an everyday sense of *caring* that concentrates on the conduct or character of the teachers, not the relation. When a teacher works conscientiously, perhaps very hard, to help her students to succeed, we often give her moral credit for caring. She seems to know what her students need, and acts faithfully on those beliefs. However, these are *assumed* needs, rather than expressed needs, and these teachers are often remembered as saying, 'Some day you'll thank me for this!' I have called such teachers 'virtue carers', contrasting their mode of teaching with that of 'relational carers': they do not establish caring relations of engage in 'caring for' as described in care ethics. As a result, their efforts to care often misfire, and the students who most need to be part of a caring relation suffer most.

I think there are few things to say about Noddings' position here. She is surely correct that teachers would want to question exhibiting (and thereby modelling) caring relationships which *only* take the form Noddings ascribes to 'virtue carers'. Such relationships, well intentioned as they may be, are enacted without attending fully to the thoughts, sentiments and goals of the students. However, it is not clear how the position can be justifiably attributed to a virtue-based approach. The virtuous agent is not an agent detached from their relationships with others. Certainly, the account of compassion I have sought to defend in this book is one which recognises, rather than dismisses, relations between human beings qua human beings. In other words, while virtues are agent-centred, Noddings neglects and therefore misrepresents their relational aspect. The virtuous teacher who is compassionate and caring *takes account* of the expressed needs of their students within their deliberations about the right course of action in a given situation. The expressed needs of others, that is, become part of the morally salient features for the virtuous agent who at the same time is aware that their imaginative reconstructions are fallible and where possible seeks to reduce these.

In their study focusing on teachers' understandings of compassion for refugee and asylum seeker children in England, Arnot et al. (2009, p. 254) found that teachers identified 'caring as the most important emotional response and often saw compassion in the sense of caring as part of their professional identity'. They cite the following response from a teacher which illustrates the sort of internal dialogue the teacher was having about what compassion meant and how it could be enacted:

> Blimey! Compassion, in my view, is trying to put yourself in the shoes of the victim,...and showing you understand or are trying to understand their position, ensuring that the victim doesn't feel at fault. I suppose showing that, as far as possible, you're on their side. I tend to show compassion by trying to relate their to experience to any experience of mine...And I think sometimes sharing...offers the victim...Can we use the word victim?... opens the door for them to share their experience. But I think compassion also has to be demonstrated through action. So it's then 'this is what I can do about it. Or if there's nothing I can do about it, this is what I can do for you...'. It's a big question isn't it?

In this extract, we can follow the reflection of the teacher about their vocabulary and the connection between compassion and what, in this situation, might form appropriate compassionate action. Crucially, this extract and a number of others reported by Arnot et al. indicate that for these teachers such reflection on compassion *included* listening to the cared-for in ways which informed deliberation and came to shape their active responses.

What is not clear from Arnot et al.'s study is the ways in which teachers' compassion provides a model for students. That is, while teachers spoke about their desire and efforts to ensure their fellow students developed and expressed compassion, we are not told how whether they understood their own compassionate responses to form part of the learning process. The exploration of such a connection would have been interesting given, and as Sanderse (2013, pp. 37–38) suggests, 'if teachers want students to emulate them, they will have to explain to students how their actions and emotional reactions are related to an ideal of the virtuous life'.

A second pedagogical approach which is frequently cited within character education literature is students' participatory action, referred to variously as social action, service learning and community involvement (to name but a few). This approach draws on the Aristotelian notion of habituation, and involves students in engaging in and subsequently reflecting on some form of action for the good of others (In making this comment I am aware of the vast literature which finds that student action is undertaken for a range of reasons, many of which are beneficial for those undertaking the action. One need not reject this evidence in order to accept that action for the good of others is at least one reason for social action, even it is one among many. This connects back to the comments made on altruistic actions offered in Chap. 4).

A body of literature now exists within and beyond moral education which explores student participatory experiences in connection with education and schooling, and while there is not space here to do full justice to this work, I do not think it controversial to suggest that one way in which schools might seek to engage students in compassionate action is through planned forms of social action in which they respond to the suffering of others and by demonstrating their solidarity. I also do not think it controversial to offer the suggestion that this action can be perceived, framed and enacted in many different ways. Indeed, in previous chapters tensions have been highlighted within education and beyond concerning the ways in which perspectives of others and support for others can be framed. Clearly, responses to others which take seriously the thoughts, feelings and goals of those suffering, and which are based on principles of solidarity and reciprocity, are better representations of compassion than those which fail to recognise the agency of others and which are dialogically and conceptually closed. One could readily point to the sorts of virtues which could be developed and enacted through positive forms of compassionate action – such as trust, humility and love, for instance – and understand these to be lacking or compromised where relationships are unequal. There is, in other words, a particular onus on schools and teachers to consider ways in which young peoples' participation can seek to embody virtuous forms of social action rather than less edifying forms of human relationships.

How then might schools and teachers go about developing these positive relationships? While many different approaches, guidelines and checklists are available to help in this regard, one which is perhaps useful so far as compassionate action is concerned was provided by a senior leader with whom I spoke in a recent study which explored the ways in which Australian high schools educate for global citizenship.[8] The senior leader taught at a large, coeducational independent school with a Christian affiliation. The senior leader was responsible for overseeing student action through the school's membership of an international organisation promoting service to others. In our discussion of activities related to education for global citizenship, social action projects were considered and the senior leader became animated in his concern about how these were focused elsewhere in the school. Drawing on his professional judgement and values, the senior leader (his views are those framed by single speech marks in what follows) had developed core criteria which as he explained were framed by a particular way of conceiving social action which prioritises solidarity and partnership. The criteria, all interconnected, were underpinned by the commitment to 'no fundraising for the sake of fundraising' and engagement only with 'community *partners*…either local or international'. For this school leader, compassionate student action only made sense if enacted through partnership and solidarity with others.

First, such engagements need to have an educational component in which students learned about and with those to whom their action is directed, with mutually beneficial understanding developing – including about interests and goals. Education here also referred to students' critical reflection on the various aspects of their social action activities and experiences. Second, social action has to be structured around student involvement in a myriad of ways. Students were therefore central to coming to recognise the suffering of others, rather than being directed to it by their teachers, making their social action more authentic expressions of compassion. Social action in which the school was involved was negotiated with other students through representation bodies, such as the student representative council, was led by students through student leadership programs, and its outcomes were disseminated to the wider student body. Central here is the rejection and avoidance of what Cartwright (2008) refers to as compulsory compassion, a process which focuses on action with the absence of the associated feeling. In such situations, as Cartwright (2008, p. 47) explains it: 'I may act on the demand even if I do not feel really compelled in my heart to do so, because I believe others would expect me to.'

Third, and crucially, all planned social action activities were subject to a timeframe of at least 5 years. As the senior leader explained 'we're not going to say, well this year we'll do this, well next year let's go to here. If we commit ourselves to a partner, it's a 5-year partnership which has set goals. The aim should be to try and achieve sustainability in that project.' In this way, social action was sustainable in ways which not only drew in future cohorts of students, but also worked to develop deeper partnerships and levels of reciprocal understanding and attachment. These practices in this particular school, within which relevant virtues are at times implicit and at others explicit, seek to limit the extent to which students' social action engendered in response to the suffering of others may fall into activities proposed as 'a way to act to rid oneself of guilt, and of obligation itself, cheaply and without genuine involvement in the situation of the unfortunates suffering' (Boltanski 1999, p. 18). Through the criteria the school leader was working to frame students' responses to suffering in particular ways – ways which incorporated notions of solidarity and partnership and which required students to engage deeply with the various features of their compassionate action.

To summarise this section, recognising that educating character involves a range of processes relating to wider school life and including teacher relationships it has been suggested that cultivating compassion requires an *explicit* approach drawing on a composite of processes and practices through which various components of compassion can be explored, developed and expressed. Central to such approaches are the use of a moral vocabulary of compassion through which relationships, values and actions can be framed, reflected on and refined. In the next section these sentiments are developed further in connection to a further, crucial aspect of the moral work of schools; namely, partnerships with families and communities.

FAMILIES AND COMMUNITIES

The focus of this section is on the relationships between schools, families and communities as they relate to compassion. My plan here is not to bemoan a lack of compassion and extol the need for ever more levels compassion. As said previously, my suggestion that there is room for more compassion in our lives stems not from a deficit approach, but from the views, first, that we could all use a little more compassion in our lives, and second, that any call for more compassion must always start from appreciating that compassion is already a feature of schools, families and communities. For this reason, the educationally pertinent question changes from 'how can families and communities become compassionate' to 'in what ways are families and communities already compassionate, how is this recognised by and related to schools, and how might compassion and education for compassion be developed further?'. The framing of the question in this second sense recognises that the moral enterprise undertaken by schools does not occur in a vacuum, isolated from other sources of moral cultivation. Clearly, any form of education about and for compassion that takes places in schools will be both meaningful and successful only to the extent to which it is located within and makes connections with what is concurrently going on within families and communities. The purpose of this section, then, is to start from the assumption that just as suffering is an observable feature of young people's lives, so too is compassion. With this recognition in mind, some thoughts are offered which relate to the ways in which schools and teachers do and could draw connections with families and communities.

The first point that must be made from the outset is that families in particular, and wider communities to perhaps a lesser extent, play a more significant role in the development of young people's character than schools. Certainly this is true so far as families are concern, as is indicated by the wealth of character education literature which attests to the centrality of the family, which Mary-Ann Glendon (1995, p. 2) refers to as 'first and foremost among' the 'seedbeds of virtue' (see also, Lickona 1996; Layard and Dunn 2009; Lexmond and Reeves 2009; Arthur et al. 2015a). As Arthur (2003, pp. 146–147; emphasis added) points out, 'the family and school are at the heart of the moral economy for they, *especially when operating together*, hold out the best possibility of nurturing in the child the ability to transcend self-interest and to regard the interests of others as in some way their own'. As Arthur reminds us here, a collaborative relationship between families and schools (and we can add in communities here too) is central to the moral formation of the child. This gives pause for thought for schools regarding the ways in which the moral virtues formed and expressed *within* the school – including compassion – connect with (which may include some form of disruption) those of families and the wider communities in which they operate.

We must be aware, however, that there may be certain conditions which prevent, or at least serve to limit, a constructive relationship between schools and families so far as moral education is concerned – conditions which schools should take account of. In particular, many have identified a trend in westernised nations within which families are increasingly private units, retracted from community and public life. In their influential study in the US, Bellah and his colleagues (1996, pp. 111–112) opined the 'fact that the family is no longer an integral part of a larger moral ecology tying the individual to community, church, and nation. The family is the core of the private sphere, whose aim is not to link individuals to the public world, but to avoid it as far as possible'. We do not need to be adopt a pessimistic view of family life to accept that a range of factors place pressures on families (whatever their structure) and that these affect the ways in which families form and shape young peoples' character. In their UK-based study, Layard and Dunn (2009) remind us that while 'families vary greatly... [the] principles of loving care are the same in any family and any culture – good physical care, unconditional love and clear boundaries for behaviour'.[9] These principles of loving care for oneself and for others are central to compassion, and also would be prioritised by schools (I can think of no school which would claim not to promote principles of loving care!). Yet, how such principles are envisioned and enacted are clearly open to some sort of mismatch between intentions and their exercise in practice.

I think there are three immediate reasons why this may be the case which should be noted here for the extent to which can serve to detract from educating about and for compassion. The first reason stems from the recognition that our schools operate in certain conditions, one which over the last three decades have become characterised by neo-liberalism. According to the title of their book, Layard and Dunn (2009) suggest that we live in a 'competitive age'. Schools are crucial sites in this age, which we see through the neo-liberalisation of education and schooling within which the rhetoric of choice, competition and markets have come to dominate. Education has become increasingly conducted through policy technologies which prioritise standardised-testing and educational league-tables at local, national and global levels in the name of increasing parental choice and school/teacher effectiveness. Such conditions promote competition not just in schools, but also between schools. Moreover, they result in and in turn depend on consumerist parents who allocate their economic and cultural resources when selecting (or choosing) schools. As Ball (2003, p. 168) remarks, through these quasi-market conditions parents with higher socio-economic status become:

> fearful, alert and strategic...(and) within the social field of education the middle class have enough capitals in the right currency, to ensure a high probability of success for their children. Their tactical deployment of these capitals more often than not enables them to gain access to and monopolize advantageous educational sites and trajectories.

Under these conditions, education shifts to become a quasi-economic commodity in ways which compromise its proper categorisation as a public good provided without profit and for the general well-being of society. This shift is one through which the morals of community and collectiveness (which include compassion) become pervaded by market practices and 'values'. While the existing moral work of schools and teachers should not be underplayed, pervading structures clearly *do* impact on the ways in which moral virtues are framed, enacted and experienced. As debates regarding compassion (or the deemed lack of compassion) in healthcare professions indicates, structural constraints and cultures antithetical to empathy and care for others can serve to restrict both the formation and expression of compassion. Thus, and according to Bramley and Matiti (2014, p. 8), 'whilst the nursing profession alone is working hard to promote the importance of compassion, it is unlikely to improve the total patient experience without a whole system change, which promotes the importance of a culture of compassion through the whole of healthcare organisations'. Research evidence points to similar concerns in relation to teachers' moral work, with teachers reporting 'that they are not always given the time in the workplace to reflect on the best way to practice moral virtues' and 'confirmed that this is largely due to increasing workloads, a very prescriptive education system and a narrow focus on academic success[10]' (Arthur et al. 2015b, p. 5).

Interestingly, another study reports a correlation between student performance on moral dilemma assessment tests and institutional practices and cultures in their school which interrupt techno-rationalist educational practices. It found that in these schools teachers reported 'a higher emphasis on moral teaching', that 'teachers...felt that they could deviate from the standard curriculum without permission', and that 'teachers...felt that they had the time and flexibility to deal with moral issues as they arose' (Arthur et al. 2015a, p. 24). We must consider, therefore, the extent to which neo-liberalising forces either restrict the development of virtues or direct this development towards certain "virtues", such as the current trend towards grit and resilience (see, Duckworth 2016 for a notable example). Crucial here is the extent to which capacities cited as virtuous serve rather than disrupt neo-liberal projects.

Second, and as I have written elsewhere (Peterson 2010), any attempt to form a productive relationship between schools and families (and once again we can add communities in here too) is to a large extent dependent on whether they share, use and esteem a common *moral vocabulary* not only of character and virtues, but of the conception/s of human flourishing to which they relate. Research evidence suggests that without careful and systematic cultivation, students can experience difficulties in developing and using a moral vocabulary. A large study in England found, for example, that a 'significant aspect of the discussions with students was their apparent difficulties in understanding the language of character and values and finding their own words to express their feelings and sentiments. For example, they found it hard to make a distinction between "being good" and "being successful"' (Arthur et al. 2009).

The third reason for a possible mismatch between intention and practice connects to the first and second and has to do with the sort of relationships which can exist between teachers, families and schools. Quite simply, where such relationships are built on trust, dialogue, reciprocity and mutuality so much the better for the shared enterprise of character development. Yet, such positive foundations do not always provide the basis for interchange between these key socialising institutions. A small-scale exploratory project in which I was recently involved in Australia found that teachers (though notably not school principals) largely justified the need to teach children moral values on the basis that these were not being appropriately or sufficiently attended to within families and the wider community (Peterson and Bentley 2016). That is, these teachers considered that they were not only teaching values, but were doing so in part to compensate for what was happening (or not happening!) in families and communities. Other evidence on a larger-scale also raises concerns. Of particular relevance for our focus on compassion, a recent report from the Harvard Graduate School of Education's *Making Caring Common* project points to a lack of trust between key sources for moral education. The study reports that 'according to our teacher survey, most teachers believe they prioritize their students being caring, but that their fellow teachers don't' and that '93 % of teachers also viewed parents as putting their children's achievement or happiness ahead of concern for others' (HGSE 2014, p. 14).

Under conditions in which teachers seemingly lack confidence in the moral work of colleagues, parents and communities so far as caring for others is concerned, moral education is likely to be compromised. That is, it is not immediately clear whether, and if so how, the teachers in the survey can be said to be working in *partnership* with colleagues, families and communities when they consider colleagues and parents to be placing rather different emphases on developing care to their own. This point is not insignificant for compassion, particularly if we accept Popenoe's (1995, p. 73) contention that 'for the moral development of children, no aspect of community support is more important than the community's ability to reinforce the social expectations of parents...Young people need to hear a consistent message about right and wrong from all the important adults in their lives; they need not only a social community but a moral community'. Research evidence provided by the Jubilee Centre for Character and Virtues and Populus (2013) indicates that parents *do* expect schools to promote and instil core moral values in their children and that schooling is a moral enterprise as well as one which is academic (a view which students also express, see Arthur et al. 2014b). Of importance, then, are co-operative processes which move beyond the sorts of behavioural codes often found within home-school agreements. Indeed, home-school agreements seem an apt example of a well-intentioned practice which carries the risk of being presented in narrow terms – of value for fostering academic and economic success or for maintaining school discipline without necessarily taking into account any wider conception of virtuous lives (Yu 2004; Peterson 2010). To put it simply and to return to the focus on care to illustrate the point, we want young people to care for others not only because it might be valuable for their academic/economic success and for the conduct of schooling but also because caring for others says something about the sorts of people they are and desire to be. With compassion in mind, this requires that schools work within themselves and also with parents and communities in order to develop education about and for compassion in ways which engage with meanings, including mediating any differences regarding these. Relevant in this regard is developing responses to questions such as 'what do we conceive compassion to mean within our families, schools and communities?', 'what are the key features of this conception of compassion, and what practices illustrate it in action?', and 'what educational processes work to support young people's formation and expression of compassion so understood?'.

These questions start from the assumption that young people, and the communities in which they reside, are already experiencing – either directly or as observers – compassion itself and its various components (empathic distress, care for others etc.). Such experiences are likely to derive from engagements within schools and families, and also from young peoples' interactions with a range of community groups and organisations, including faith-groups, sports,[11] arts and social clubs, and charitable organisations.

How, then, might schools develop such engagements? In their guide *Building Character Education In Your Community*, the University of Illinois (n.d.) provide useful structural guidance in this regard for educational institutions adapted from those developed by the *Character Counts!* initiative. The resource identifies two levels for planning connections with community. At level 1, this is based around five categories: *commitment* (who needs to be involved, what the community's needs are, and building networks); *consensus* (determining core values with others, developing objectives, vision and mission through discussion); *collaborate* (workshops and training, identifying 'key leaders', developing plans based on mission and expanding networks); *collect data* (ascertaining what data would be of value, collecting this data); and, *communicate* (select dissemination sources, disseminate vision, data and practices) (University of Illinois, n.d., pp. 6–7). At level 2, there are four categories: *explore* (deciding on appropriate strategies to enact the vision within the community, join with 'existing community-wide events', connecting these with activities in school); *engage and excite* (plan activities with/within the community, hold events and practices which explore and promote core values); *expand* (further promotion of activities, extending into wider networks, build student leadership); and, *evaluate* (collect, analyse and communicate outcomes, inform further practices through evaluation data). These levels and their respective categories provide a useful structure through which schools, families and communities can reflect on, evaluate and develop further their existing work in the shared exercise of cultivating compassion.

Conclusion

The aim of this chapter has been to explore what it might mean for schools to be compassionate institutions, compassionate institutions that in which teachers take seriously their moral role and work in partnership with families and communities. Against some important contextual considerations which may manifest some sort of mismatch between intention and actual existing practices, it has been argued that compassionate schooling involves schools, families and communities working together to develop a shared sense of the good life and what their young people can become. Crucial within such working practices are teachers who accept, embrace and reflect on the moral nature of their role and whom, in doing so, render morality – and for our purposes compassion – explicit in their work. For this to occur, and following Noddings (1999, p. 215), requires an acceptance that 'teachers who, as carers, want to respond to the voiced and unvoiced needs of their students must have what might be called latitudinal knowledge. They should be able to draw on literature, history, politics, religion, philosophy and the arts in ways that enrich their daily teaching and offer multiple possibilities for students to make connections with the great existential questions as well as questions of current social life'.

With this in mind, in concluding this chapter it would be remiss not to say something about the preparation of teachers. Most literature on character education points to two fundamental concerns regarding preparing teachers as moral educators (see, e.g., Carr 1991; Kristjànsson 2015; Arthur et al. 2015b): (1) recognising that teachers are moral educators and need preparation in this regard, and (2) the reductionism of teacher preparation programmes and the resulting contraction of engagement with philosophical, theological, psychological, historical and sociological ideas on morality and education. Both of these concerns are expressed succinctly in the recommendations of a recent report on teachers and character education in the UK, which calls for initial teacher education programmes and ongoing teacher professional development to 'focus on developing the moral agency of teachers, resisting the tendency to adhere to a reductive, formulaic model of teaching' and argues that 'making space for ethical reflection on practice and developing understanding of character education are two priorities' (Arthur et al. 2015b, p. 5). Such focus and resistance is crucial if teachers are to appreciate the moral nature of their work and the ways this extends to partnerships with colleagues, families and communities.

NOTES

1. http://www.charterforcompassion.org/index.php/charter-for-compassio
nate-schools; emphasis in original.
2. http://www.creatingcompassionatecultures.org/the-seven-steps.html

3. https://www.pshe-association.org.uk/curriculum-and-resources/resources/ten-principles-effective-pshe-education
4. All UK-based awarding bodies offering programmes and qualifications.
5. For a survey of empirical literature on role-modelling see Sanderse 2013.
6. The use of the term emulate rather than imitate is deliberate, given the former includes the bringing of the observed and valued virtue into the character of the child in a critical way. The term imitation seems to denote mere mimicry. Kristjànsson (2015) draws on the Aristotelian notion of 'emulation' with regard to the process through which young people can come to learn from the virtues of others. As Sanderse (2013, p. 36) also suggests emulation involves greater educative depth than imitation, and moves the child from 'becoming like the teacher' to 'becoming like what the teacher exemplifies'.
7. A list of 24 character strengths based on the Values in Action inventory developed by Peterson and Seligman (2004) and Peterson and Park (2009).
8. ARC DE150100926 'How Australian High Schools Educate for Global Citizenship'.
9. In his recent detailed sociological exploration of the family as it relates to the community in the USA, Robert Putnam (2015) draws some interesting pictures of contemporary forms of family, including the impact of increasing work pressures.
10. A separate study from the Jubilee Centre for Character and Virtues reports that 'as competition and accountability increase, the gap between professional altruistic motivations and working practices conducive to such motives increases. Teachers in this study were pleased to have the opportunity to discuss issues of character and virtue, arguing that these had been squeezed out of discourse by the predominance of quasi-accountability measures. The apparently relentless focus on technique, audit trails and assessment risks endangering the enthusiasm and goodwill of teachers found in this study. The finding that colleagues provide support and in some ways ameliorate the stress of such demands highlights the importance of such relationships in good teaching practice'.
11. It has been assumed that participation in sports clubs provided a platform for the development of character, but recent research found no correlation between such engagement and performance on moral dilemma-based assessments (Arthur et al. 2015a). More evidence is needed which examines this further, and so participation in sports clubs is included here with this proviso. The same study did find a correlation with participation in music, choir and drama-based activities.

CONCLUDING THOUGHTS

My aim in this book has been to set out and defend the importance of compassion from a virtue-based perspective, and to make connections between these arguments and the cultivation of compassion in schools. Incorporating the empirical suggestion that human suffering is a visible part of our everyday lived experiences, the main arguments of this book have been as follows:

1. Compassion as a virtue can be understood as a cognitive and emotional response to the suffering of others. Compassion is based on a recognition and appreciation of common humanity, including humanity's fragility. It requires empathy, care for others and can inform and lead to actions in support of others. Compassion represents an expression of ourselves and our humanity, and relates to notions of the good life and human flourishing;

2. Educating about and for compassion connects young people to others and their communities, asking and supporting them to develop empathic, caring and altruistic responses to others on the basis of common humanity. Compassion provides a disposition vital for living and working with others. In this way, developing compassion can help young people to make a positive contribution to their schools and communities;

3. Any educational approach to cultivating compassion starts from the following acknowledgements: (1) that young people, schools, teachers, families and communities will already be compassionate in particular

© The Author(s) 2017
A. Peterson, *Compassion and Education*,
DOI 10.1057/978-1-137-54838-2

ways. Appreciating these ways provides an important foundation for cultivating compassion further; (2) cultivating compassion is a process involving a combination of explicit taught and often implicit caught practices. The former relates most closely to the formal curriculum, but also involves teachers responding to issues of concern to young people and/or engaging with current issues. The latter includes a range of processes, included school ethos, culture, values, extra-curricular activities, and student–teacher/teacher–teacher relationships; (3) cultivating compassion through education and schooling will be more effective when conducted through mutual, reciprocal and trustful relationships between schools, teachers, families and communities; (4) the structures, discourses and values which shape educational practices will not always be conducive for compassion, and indeed in important ways may seek to work against it. This requires educators to be cognisant of competing discourses in order to work against those which limit compassion; (5) underpinning each of these is particular and shared moral vocabulary through which those involved can explore key notions of compassion – including its relationship with human flourishing;

4. How schools and teachers conceive compassion and its necessary components will inform and shape the ways it is (and indeed is not) included within all aspects of schools. This suggests that not only should teachers – in partnership with families and communities – explore what compassion means, but that they should give thought to how they understand their own roles as moral educators, including the moral vocabulary they use.

To close, I would like to offer the following reflection. In recent times, particularly but not only in England, there has been something of a revival of interest in educating for virtues, a revival which has impacted a great deal on educational policy and practice. It will not come as a surprise to readers of this book that in broad terms I believe that this revival is to be very much welcomed. There is though, a note of caution – one which becomes clear when we remember that character education is not a homogenous discipline, and can be put to work in some very different ways (Kristjánsson 2015). Of particular reason for caution is the predominance of interest, particularly amongst politicians and policy makers, in certain pseudo-virtues such as grit and resilience. When character education becomes characterised by such terms it misses the mark. As Jeffrey Snyder (2014) suggests, character becomes 'treated as a kind of fuel that will help propel students through school and up the career ladder'. Educating for moral virtues, such as compassion, may well lead students to greater achievements within school and in their careers – but that is not its primary point, purpose nor motivation. Rather, educating for moral virtues aims at cultivating better human beings qua human beings and, by extension, more caring schools and communities. In this endeavour narrowly defined academic and economic achievements remain secondary – an added bonus, rather than the motivating factor. When we recognise that the compassionate life is one involving virtue, and that the virtuous life is one which promotes human flourishing (our own and that of others), the motivation necessary for compassion – and cultivating compassion in schools – is already provided.

REFERENCES

Andreotti, V. (2006). Soft versus critical global citizenship education. *Policy & Practice – A Development Education Review*. Issue 3. http://www.developmen teducationreview.com/issue3-focus4. Accessed 1 May 2015.

Annas, J. (2011). *Intelligent virtue*. Oxford: Oxford University Press.

Appiah, K. A. (2007). *Cosmopolitanism: Ethics in a world of strangers*. London: Penguin.

Arendt, H. (1963). *On revolution*. London: Penguin Books.

Aristotle. (2009). *The Nichomachean ethics*. Oxford: Oxford University Press.

Aristotle. (2012). *The art of rhetoric*. London: Collins Classics.

Armstrong, K. (2011). *Twelve steps to a compassionate life*. London: The Bodley Head.

Arnot, M., Pinson, H., & Candappa, M. (2009). Compassion, caring and justice: Teachers' strategies to maintain moral integrity in the face of national hostility to the 'non-citizen'. *Educational Review, 61*(3), 249–264.

Arthur, J. (2003). *Education with character: The moral economy of schooling*. London: Routledge.

Arthur, J., Harding, R., & Godfrey, R. (2009). *Citizens of character: The values and character dispositions of 14–16 year olds in the hodge hill constituency*. A report for the Templeton Foundation. Canterbury: Learning for Life.

Arthur, J., Harrison, T., Carr, D., Kristjánsson, K., Davison, I., with Hayes, D., Higgins, J. and Davison, J. (2014a). *Knightly virtues: Enhancing virtue literacy through stories*. Birmingham: Jubilee Centre for Character and Virtues.

Arthur, J., Harrison, T., Kristjánsson, K., Davison, I., with Hayes, D., & Higgins, J. (2014b). *My character: Enhancing future-mindedness in young people: a feasibility study*. Birmingham: Jubilee Centre for Character and Virtues.

Arthur, J., Kristjànsson, K., Walker, D., Sanderse, W., Jones, C. with Thoma, S., Curren, R. and Roberts, M. (2015a). *Character education in UK schools: Research report*. Birmingham: Jubilee Centre for Character and Virtues.

Arthur, J., Kristjànsson, K., Cooke, S., Brown, E., & Carr, D. (2015b). *The good teacher: Understanding virtues in practice*. Birmingham: Jubilee Centre for Character and Virtues.

Arthur, J., Harrison, T., & Wright, D. (eds.). (n.d.). *Teaching character through the curriculum: A guide to educating the virtues through and within 14 secondary school subjects*. Birmingham: Jubilee Centre for Character and Virtues.

Athanassoulis, N. (2000). A response to Harman: Virtue ethics and character traits. *Proceedings of the Aristotelian Society, 100*, 215–221.

Australian Associated Press. (2014, July 12). Stopping the boats compassionate: Abbott. *The Advertiser*. Online edition. http://www.adelaidenow.com.au/news/breaking-news/stopping-the-boats-compassionate-abbott/news-story/cecd687a724bcb220c6fd8998109f7f1?=#itm=newscomau%7Cnews%7Cncam-story-body-link%7C4%7Chttp%3A%2F%2Fwww.adelaidenow.com.au%2Fnews%2Fbreaking-news%2Fstopping-the-boats-compassionate-abbott%2Fstory-fni6ul2m-1226986560892%7Cstory%7CStopping%20the%20boats%20'compassionate'%3A%20Abbott&itmt=1457028289399. Accessed 14 Oct 2015.

Australian Government. (2005). *National framework for values education in Australian schools*. Canberra: Australian Government.

Baccalaureate, I. (2013). *What is an IB education?* Cardiff: International Baccalaureate.

Baehr, J. (2011). *The inquiring mind: The intellectual virtues and virtue epistemology*. Oxford: Oxford University Press.

Ball, S. (2003). *Class strategies and the education market: The middle class and social advantage*. London: Routledge.

Barber, B. (1984). *Strong democracy. Participatory politics for a new age*. Berkeley: University of California.

Barber, B. (1998). *A passion for democracy: American essays*. Princeton, NJ: Princeton University Press.

Barber, B. (2003). *Strong democracy. Participatory politics for a new age. 20th Anniversary Edition*. Berkeley: University of California.

Barren, P. (2015, April 2). Compassion out of cruelty. *The Northern Echo*. Online edition. http://www.thenorthernecho.co.uk/features/12869878.Compassion_out_of_cruelty/. Accessed 14 Oct 2015.

Batson, C. D. (1991). *The altruism question: Toward a social-psychological answer*. Hillsdale: Lawrence Erlbaum.

Batson, C. D. (1994). Why act for the public good? Four answers. *Personality and Social Psychology Bulletin: Special Issue: The Self and the Collective, 20*(5), 603–610.

Baughan, E., & Fiori, J. (2015). Save the children, the humanitarian project, and the politics of solidarity: Reviving Dorothy Buxton's vision. *Disastor's, 39*(2), 129–145.

Baumeister, R. F., Campbell, J. D., Krueger, J. I., & Vohs, K. D. (2003). Does high self-esteem cause better performance, interpersonal success, happiness, or healthier lifestyles? *Psychological Science in the Public Interest, 4*, 1–44.

Bausells, M. (2015, August 24, Monday). Calais migrant camp gets makeshift library – and it needs more books. *The Guardian*, Online Edition. http://www.theguardian.com/books/2015/aug/24/calais-migrant-camp-gets-makeshift-library-and-it-needs-more-books. Accessed 16 Feb 2016.

Bekkers, R., & Wiepking, P. (2011). A literature review of empirical studies of philanthropy: Eight mechanisms that drive charitable giving. *Nonprofit and Voluntary Sector Quarterly, 40*(5), 924–973.

Bellah, R. N., Madsen, R., Sullivan, W. M., Swidler, A., & Tipton, S. M. (Eds.). (1996). *Habits of the heart: Individualism and commitment in American life*. Berkeley: University of California.

Benhabib, S. (1996). Toward a deliberative model of democratic legitimacy. In S. Benhabib (Ed.), *Democracy and difference: Contesting the boundaries of the political* (pp. 67–94). Princeton: Princeton University Press.

Ben-Ze'Ev, A. (2000). *The subtlety of emotions*. London: MIT Press.

Berlant, L. (2004). Introduction: Compassion (and withholding). In L. Berlant (Ed.), *Compassion: The culture and politics of an emotion* (pp. 1–14). London: Routledge.

Bertram, C. (2010). Why Rousseau still matters. *The Philosopher's Magazine, 47*, 34–42.

Blair, T. (2015, May 9). Labour must be the party of ambition as well as compassion. *The Guardian*. http://www.theguardian.com/commentisfree/2015/may/09/tony-blair-what-labour-must-do-next-election-ed-miliband. Accessed 15 Oct 2015.

Blum, L. (1987). Compassion. In R. B. Kruschwitz and R. C. Roberts (Eds.), *The virtues: Essays on moral character* (pp. 229–236). Belmont: Wandsworth.

Bluth, K., & Blanton, P. W. (2014). The influence of self-compassion on emotional well-being among early and older adolescent males and females. *Journal of Positive Psychology*. doi:10.1080/17439760.2014.936967

Boli, J. (2005). Contemporary developments in world culture. *International Journal of Comparative Sociology, 45*(5–6), 383–404.

Body, A., & Breeze, B. (2016). What are 'unpopular causes' and how can they achieve fundraising success? *International Journal of Nonprofit and Voluntary Sector Marketing, 21*(1), 57–70.

Bohlin, K. (2005). *Teaching character education through literature: Awakening the moral imagination in secondary classrooms*. London: Routledge.

Boler, M. (1999). *Feeling power: Emotions and education*. New York: Routledge.

Boltanski, L. (1999). *Distant suffering: Morality, media and politics*. Cambridge: Cambridge University Press.

Borg, M. J. (1997). *The God we never knew: Beyond dogmatic religion to a more authentic contemporary faith*. San Francisco: HarperCollins.

Boyd, R. (2004). Pity's pathologies portrayed: Rousseau and the limits of democratic compassion. *Political Theory, 32*(4), 519–546.

Bradshaw, L. (2008). Emotions, reasons and judgements. In R. Kingston and L. Ferry (Eds.), *Bringing the passions back in: The emotions in political philosophy.* Vancouver, BC: UBC Press.

Bramley, L., & Matiti, M. (2014). How does it really feel to be in my shoes? Patient's experiences of compassion within nursing care and their perceptions of developing compassionate nurses. *Journal of Clinical Nursing, 23*(19–20), 1–10.

British Broadcasting Corporation. (1999, July 22, Thursday). Medical cannabis grower acquitted. http://news.bbc.co.uk/1/hi/health/401186.stm. Accessed 16 Feb 2016.

British Broadcasting Corporation. (2015a, May 12). Cameron tells cabinet to focus on opportunity and compassion. http://www.bbc.co.uk/news/uk-politics-32700111. Accessed 15 Oct 2015.

British Broadcasting Corporation. (2015b, May 3). Nepal quake: Airport customs holding up aid relief – UN. http://www.bbc.co.uk/news/world-asia-32564891. Accessed 15 Oct 2015.

British Broadcasting Corporation. (2015c, June 15, Monday). *Beyond belief: Compassion.*

British Broadcasting Corporation. (2016, May 25, Tuesday). *Storyville: Last days in Vietnam..*

Byrne, L. (2015, October 29). Why doesn't the government think 'compassion' is a British value?. *The New Statesman.* http://www.newstatesman.com/politics/education/2015/10/why-doesnt-government-think-compassion-british-value. Accessed 16 Feb 2016.

Callan, E. (1988). The moral status of pity. *Canadian Journal of Philosophy, 18*(1), 1–12.

Carr, D. (1991). *Educating the virtues: Essay on the philosophical psychology of moral development and education.* London: Routledge.

Carr, D. (2015). Is gratitude a moral virtue? *Philosophical Studies, 172*(6), 1475–1484.

Carr, D., & Harrison, T. (2015). *Educating character through stories.* Exeter: Imprint Academic.

Cartwright, L. (2008). *Moral spectatorship: Technologies of voice and affect in postwar representations of the child.* London: Duke University Press.

Cassell, E. J. (2002). Compassion. In C. Snyder & S. J. Lopez (Eds.), *Handbook of positive psychology* (pp. 434). Oxford: Oxford University Press.

Cayton, P. (2011). *Compassion in education: An introduction to creating compassionate cultures.* London: Foundation for Developing Wisdom and Compassion.

Chazan, E. J. (1998). *The moral self.* London: Routeldge.

Chazan, P. (1993). Rousseau as a psycho-social moralist: The distinction between Amour De Soi and Amour-Propre. *History of Philosophy Quarterly, 10*(4), 341–354.

Clark, C. (1997). *Misery and company: Sympathy in everyday life*. Chicago: The University of Chicago Press.

Clary, E. G., & Miller, J. (1986). Socialization and situational influences on sustained altruism. *Child Development, 57*, 1358–1369.

Coles, M. I. (2015a). Changing the story, altering the paradigm. In M. I. Coles (Ed.), *Towards the compassionate school* (pp. 1–22). London: IOE Press.

Coles, M. I. (2015b). Conclusion: Bringing it all together – The next steps. In M. I. Coles (Ed.), *Towards the compassionate school* (pp. 122–124). London: IOE Press.

Comte-Sponville, A. (2003). *A short treatise on the great virtues: The uses of philosophy in everyday life*. London: Vintage.

Crisp, R. (2008). Compassion and beyond. *Ethical Theory and Moral Practice, 11*(3), 233–246.

Daniel, N. (2013, January 10). Teaching children empathy. *Women's Hour*. BBC Radio Four.

Darley, J. M., & Batson, C. D. (1973). From Jerusalem to Jericho: A study of situational and dispositional variables in helping behaviour. *Journal of Psychology and Social Psychology, 27*(1), 100–108.

Darley, J. M., & Latané, B. (1968). Bystander intervention in emergencies: Diffusion of responsibility. *Journal of Personality and Social Psychology, 8*(4), 377–383.

Dathan, M. (2015, September 3). Aylan Kurdi: David Cameron says he felt 'deeply moved' by images of dead Syrian boy but gives no details of plans to take in more refugees. *The Independent*. Online edition. http://www.independent.co.uk/news/uk/politics/aylan-kurdi-david-cameron-says-he-felt-deeply-moved-by-images-of-dead-syrian-boy-but-gives-no-10484641.html. Accessed 14 Oct 2015.

Davies, O. (2010). *A theology of compassion: Metaphysics of difference and the renewal of tradition*. Cambridge: William B. Eerdmans Publishing Company.

Davison, M. (2015). Compassionate care – a superpower or just part of the job?. *The Guardian*. Online edition. http://www.theguardian.com/healthcare-network/2015/feb/17/nursing-nhs-compassionate-care-job-challenge. Accessed 18 Mar 2016.

Dewey, J. (1933). *How we think*. London: D. C. Heath.

De Waal, F. (2006). *Primates and philosophers: How morality evolved*. New Jersey: Princeton University Press.

Dearden, L. (2015, April 21). Tony Abbott tells Europe to 'stop the boats' like Australia as migrant crisis continues. *The Independent*. Online edition. http://www.independent.co.uk/news/world/europe/tony-abbott-tells-europe-to-stop-the-boats-like-australia-as-migrant-crisis-continues-10191566.html. Accessed 30 Apr 2015.

Dekker, P., & Halman, L. (2003). Volunteering and values: An introduction. In P. Dekker & L. Halman (Eds.), *The values of volunteering: Cross-cultural perspectives* (pp. 1–18). New York: Springer.

Dent, N. J. H. (1988). *Rousseau: An Introduction to his psychological, social and political theory.* Oxford: Basil Blackwell.

Dent, N. J. H. (1998). Rousseau on amour-propre. *Proceedings of the Aristotelian Society. Supplementary Volumes, 72,* 57–73.

Department for Education. (2016). *Education excellence everywhere.* London: DfE.

Department of Health. (2012). *Compassion in practice: Nursing, Midwifery and care staff – our vision and strategy.* London: Department of Health.

Devichand, M. (2016, January 2). Alan Kurdi's aunt: 'My dead nephew's picture saved thousands of lives. BBC online. http://www.bbc.co.uk/news/blogs-trending-35116022. Accessed 20 Feb 2016.

Dill, J. S. (2013). *The longings and limits of global citizenship education: The moral pedagogy of schooling in a cosmopolitan Age.* New York: Routledge.

Dobson, A. (2006). Thick cosmopolitanism. *Political Studies, 54,* 165–184.

Doherty, B. (2014, December 30). Stopping the boats' a fiction as Australia grows ever more isolationist on asylum. *The Guardian.* Online edition. http://www.theguardian.com/australia-news/2014/dec/31/stopping-the-boats-a-fiction-as-australia-grows-ever-more-isolationist-on-asylum. Accessed 14 Apr 2015.

Doris, J. M. (1998). Persons, situations, and virtue ethics. *Nous, 32,* 504–530.

Dower, N. (1991). World poverty. In P. Singer (Ed.), *A companion to ethics.* Oxford: Oxford University Press.

Duckworth, A. (2016). *Grit: The power of passion and perseverance.* New York: Simon and Schuster.

Ehlert, J., Ehlert, N., & Merrens, M. (1973). The influence of ideological affiliation on helping behaviour. *Journal of Social Psychology, 89,* 315–316.

Eisenberg, N. (1986). *Altruistic cognition, emotion and behavior.* Hillsdale: Erlbaum.

Eisenberg, N., & Miller, P. A. (1987). The relation of empathy to prosocial and related behaviors. *Psychological Bulletin, 101*(1), 91–119.

Eisenberg, N., Spinrad, T. L., & Savdovsky, A. (2006). Empathy-related responding in children. In M. Killen & J. Smetana (Eds.), *Handbook of moral development.* Mahwah: Lawrence Erlbaum Associates.

Faulkner, N. (2014a). Compassion and the stolen generations. In M. Ure & M. Frost (Eds.), *The politics of compassion* (pp. 139–157). London: Routledge.

Faulkner, N. (2014b). Guilt, anger and compassionate helping. In M. Ure & M. Frost (Eds.), *The politics of compassion* (pp. 139–157). London: Routledge.

Felderhof, M., & Thompson, P. (eds.). (2014). *Teaching virtue: the contribution of religious education.* Bloomsbury: London.

Figley, C. R. (1995). *Compassion fatigue: Coping with secondary traumatic stress disorder in those who treat the traumatized.* New York: Brunner/Mazel.

Francis, R. (2013). *Report of the mid-Staffordshire NHS foundation trust public inquiry.* London: The Stationary Office.

Fraser, N. (2005, November/December). Reframing justice in a globalizing world. *New Left Review, 36,* 1–19.

Gansberg, M. (1964, March 27). 37 who saw murder didn't call the police. *New York Times.* http://www.nytimes.com/1964/03/27/37-who-saw-mhttps://theconversation.com/the-21st-century-bystander-effect-happens-every-day-online-27496urder-didnt-call-the-police.html?_r=1. Accessed 16 Feb 2016.

Garber, M. (2004). Compassion. In L. Berlant (Ed.), *Compassion: The culture and politics of an emotion.* New York: Routledge.

Garner, R. (2014). Being compassionate. In M. Felderhof & P. Thompson (Eds.), *Teaching virtue: The contribution of religious education* (pp. 86–99). London: Bloomsbury.

Gergen, K., Gergen, M., & Meter, K. (1972). Individual orientations to prosocial behaviour. *Journal of Social Issues, 28,* 105–130.

Germer, C. K., & Neff, K. D. (2013). Self-compassion in clinical practice. *Journal of Clinical Psychology: In Session, 69*(8), 856–867.

Glendon, M. A. (1995). Forgotten questions. In M. A. Glendon (Ed.), *Seedbeds of virtue: Sources of competence, character and citizenship in American society* (pp. 1–16). Lanham: Madison Books.

Goetz, J. L., Keltner, D., & Simon-Thomas, E. (2010). Compassion: An evolutionary analysis and empirical review. *Psychological Bulletin, 136,* 351–374.

Goodin, R. (2003a). Democratic deliberation within. In J. S. Fishkin & P. Laslett (Eds.), *Debating deliberative democracy* (pp. 54–79). Blackwell: Oxford.

Goodin, R. (2003b). *Reflective democracy.* Oxford: Oxford University Press.

The Guardian. (2015a, May 17). UKIP should be more compassionate says party deputy. http://www.theguardian.com/politics/2015/may/17/ukip-more-compassionate-suzanne-evans. Accessed 14 Oct 2015.

The Guardian. (2015b, September 22). Letters: Our duty in central Europe is to show compassion to refugees. http://www.theguardian.com/world/2015/sep/22/our-duty-in-central-europe-is-to-show-compassion-to-refugees. Accessed 14 Oct 2015.

Harcourt, E. (2011). Self-love and practical rationality. In C. Bagnoli (Ed.), *Morality and the emotions* (pp. 82–94). Oxford: Oxford University Press.

Harman, G. (1999). Moral philosophy meets social psychology. *Proceedings of the Aristotelian Society, 99,* 315–331.

Harth, N. S., Kessler, T., & Leach, C. W. (2008). Advantaged group's emotional response to intergroup inequality: The dynamics of pride, guilt and sympathy. *Personality & Social Psychology Bulletin, 34*(1), 115–129.

Harvard Graduate School of Education (2014). *The children we mean to raise: The real messages adults are sending about values.* Harvard: Harvard Graduate School of Education.

Haynes, F. (1998). *The ethical school: Consequences, consistency and caring.* London: Routledge.

Health Service Ombudsman. (2011). *Care and compassion.* London: The Stationary Office.

Heffernan, M., Griffen, M., McNulty, R., & Fitzpatrick, J. (2010). Self-compassion and emotional intelligence. *International Journal of Nursing Practice, 16*(4), 366–373.

Held, D. (2005). *Debating globalization.* Cambridge: Polity Press.

Held, D. (2010). *Cosmopolitanism: Ideas and realities.* Cambridge: Polity Press.

Hess, D. (2009). *Controversy in the classroom: The democratic power of discussion.* New York: Routledge.

Hickling-Hudson, A. (2011). Teaching to disrupt preconceptions: Education for social justice in the imperial aftermath. *Compare: A Journal of Comparative and International Education, 41*(4), 453–465.

Hoffman, M. L. (2000). *Empathy and moral development: Implications for caring and justice.* Cambridge: Cambridge University Press.

Holdsworth, C. (2010). Why volunteer? Understanding motivations for student volunteering. *British Journal of Educational Studies, 58*(4), 421–437.

Home Office and Department for Communities and Local Government. (2015). Syrian refugees: What you can do to help. https://www.gov.uk/government/news/syria-refugees-what-you-can-do-to-help–2. Accessed 16 Feb 2016.

Homiak, M. L. (1981). Virtue and self-love in Aristotle's ethics. *Canadian Journal of Philosophy, 11*(4), 633–651.

Hurst, D., & Doherty, B. (2016, February 2, Tuesday). High court upholds Australia's right to detain asylum seekers offshore. *The Guardian.* Online Edition. http://www.theguardian.com/australia-news/2016/feb/03/high-court-upholds-australias-right-to-detain-asylum-seekers-offshore. Accessed 16 Feb 2016.

International Baccalaureate (2013). IB learner profile. http://www.ibo.org/contentassets/fd82f70643ef4086b7d3f292cc214962/learner-profile-en.pdf. Accessed 24 May 2016.

Iyer, A., & Leach, C. W. (2010). Helping disadvantaged out-groups challenge unjust inequalities: The role of group-based emotions. In S. Stürmer & M. Snyder (Eds.), *The psychology of prosocial behavior: Group processes, intergroup relations and helping* (pp. 337–354). Oxford: Wiley Blackwell.

Iyer, A., Schmader, T., & Lickel, B. (2007). Why individuals protest the perceived transgressions of their countries: The role of anger, shame, and guilt. *Personality & Social Psychology Bulletin, 33*(4), 572–587.

Jabour, B. (2015, April 26, Sunday). Bali Nine: Julie Bishop again puts the case for clemency to Indonesian counterpart. *The Guardian,* Online Edition. http://www.theguardian.com/world/2015/apr/26/bali-nine-julie-bishop-again-puts-case-for-clemency-to-indonesian-counterpart. Accessed 15 Oct 2015.

Jackson, R. (2009). The interpretive approach to religious education and the development of a community of practice. http://wrap.warwick.ac.uk/2928/1/WRAP_Jackson_Jackson_CoP_2009_chapter1-2158.pdf. Accessed 30 Aug 2015.

Jackson, R. (2012). The interpretive approach as a research tool: Inside the REDCo project. In R. Jackson (Ed.), *Religion, education, dialogue and conflict: Perspectives on religious education research* (pp. 84–102). London: Routledge.

Joinson, C. (1992). Coping with compassion fatigue. *Nursing, 22*(4), 118–121.

Jones, C. (2002). *Global justice: Defending cosmopolitanism.* Oxford: Oxford University Press.

Jones, K. (2006). Giving and volunteering as distinct forms of civic engagement: The role of community integration and personal resources in formal helping. *Nonprofit and Voluntary Sector Quarterly, 35*(2), 249–266.

Joseph, S. (2015). Operation sovereign borders, offshore detention and the 'drownings argument'. *The Conversation.* https://theconversation.com/operation-sovereign-borders-offshore-detention-and-the-drowningsargument-45095. Accessed 25 May 2016.

Jubilee Centre for Character and Virtues. (2013). *A framework for character education in schools.* http://jubileecentre.ac.uk/userfiles/jubileecentre/pdf/other-centre-papers/Framework.pdf. Accessed 15 May 2016.

Jubilee Centre for Character and Virtues/Populus. (2013). *A framework for character education: Jubilee centre parents' survey.* http://jubileecentre.ac.uk/userfiles/jubileecentre/pdf/character-education/Populus%20Parents%20Study%20-%20short.pdf. Accessed 15 May 2016.

King, M. L. (1967). Beyond Vietnam. Speech made on 4 April. http://kingencyclopedia.stanford.edu/encyclopedia/documentsentry/doc_beyond_vietnam/. Accessed 16 Feb 2016.

Kinnick, K. N., Krugman, D. M., & Cameron, G. T. (2015). Compassion fatigue and the elusive quest for journalistic impact: A content and reader-metrics analysis assessing audience response. *Journalism & Mass Communication Quarterly, 73*(3), 700–722.

Kolodny, N. (2010). The explanation of amour-propre. *Philosophical Review, 119*(2), 165–200.

Konstan, D. (2014). Pity, compassion and forgiveness. In M. Ure & M. Frost (Eds.), *The politics of compassion* (pp. 179–188). London: Routledge.

Kristjánsson, K. (2007). *Aristotle, emotions and education.* Farnham: Ashgate.

Kristjánsson, K. (2010). Valuing the self. In T. Lovat, R. Toomey, & N. Clement (Eds.), *International research handbook on values education and student well-being* (pp. 179–194). Rotterdam: Springer.

Kristjánsson, K. (2014). Pity: A mitigated defence. *Canadian Journal of Philosophy, 44*(3-4), 343–364.

Kristjánsson, K. (2015). *Aristotelian character education*. London: Routledge.

Krznaric, R. (2008). *You are therefore I am: How empathy education can create social change*. London: Oxfam.

Lama, D. (2003). *Transforming the mind: Teachings on generating compassion*. London: Thorsons.

Lamb, R. B. (1974). Adam Smith's system: Sympathy not self-interest. *Journal of the History of Ideas, 35*(4), 671–682.

Latané, B., & Dabbs, J. M. (1975). Sex, group size and helping in three cities. *Sociometry, 38*, 180–194.

Latané, B., & Nida, S. (1981). Ten years of research on group size and helping. *Psychological Bulletin, 89*, 308–324.

Laurent, O. (2015, September 4). What the image of Aylan Kurdi says about the power of photography. *Time*. Online edition. http://time.com/4022765/aylan-kurdi-photo/. Accessed 14 Oct 2015.

Layard, R., & Dunn, J. (2009). *A good childhood: Searching for values in a competitive age*. London: Penguin.

Lee, H. (1960). *To kill a mockingbird*. London: Arrow Books.

Lexmond, J., & Reeves, R. (2009). *Building character*. London: Demos.

Lickel, B., Steele, R. R., & Schmader, T. (2011). Group-based shame and guilt: Emerging directions in research. *Social and Personality Psychology Compass, 5*(3), 153–163.

Lickona, T. (1996). Eleven principles of effective character education. *Journal of Moral Education, 25*(1), 93–100.

Lickona, T. (2004). *Character matters*. New York: Touchstone.

Lilius, J. M., Worline, M. C., Dutton, J. E., Kanov, J. M., & Maitlis, S. (2011). Understanding compassion capability. *Human Relations, 64*(7), 873–899.

Lim, D., & DeSteno, D. (2016). Suffering and compassion: The links among adverse life experiences, empathy, compassion and prosocial behaviour. *Emotion, 16*(2), 175–182.

Linklater, A. (1998). *The transformation of political community*. Cambridge: Polity Press.

Linklater, A. (2006). Cosmopolitanism. In A. Dobson & R. Eckersley (Eds.), *Political theory and the ecological challenge*. Cambridge: Cambridge University Press.

Linklater, A. (2007a). Distant suffering and cosmopolitan obligations. *International Politics, 44*, 19–36.

Linklater, A. (2007b). Towards a sociology of global morals with an 'emancipatory intent'. *Review of International Studies, 33*, 135–150.

Linklater, A. (2014). Towards a sociology of compassion in world politics. In M. Ure & M. Frost (Eds.), *The politics of compassion* (pp. 65–81). London: Routledge.

Lloyd, J. (2015). Compassion through development of physical and mental health and well-being. In M. I. Coles (Ed.), *Towards the compassionate school* (pp. 95–107). London: IOE Press.

Lu, C. (2000). The one and many faces of cosmopolitanism. *The Journal of Political Philosophy, 8*(2), 244–267.

Luther King Jr., M. (1964). Beyond Vietnam – A time to break silence. http://www.americanrhetoric.com/speeches/mlkatimetobreaksilence.htm. Accessed 24 March 2016.

Macdonald, T. (2014). Cosmopolitan political institutions. In M. Ure & M. Frost (Eds.), *The politics of compassion* (pp. 82–96). London: Routledge.

Marks, J. (2007). Rousseau's discriminating defense of compassion. *American Political Science Review, 101*(4), 727–739.

Marks, K. (1998, April 3, Friday). Jury clears man accused of growing cannabis. *The Independent.* http://www.independent.co.uk/news/jury-clears-man-accused-of-growing-cannabis-1154226.html. Accessed 19 Feb 2016.

Marshall, S. L., Parker, P. D., Ciarrochi, J., Sahdra, B., Jackson, C. J., & Heaven, P. C. L. (2015). Self-compassion protects against negative effects of low self-esteem: A longitudinal study in a large adolescent sample. *Personality and Individual Difference, 74*, 116–121.

Merry, M., & De Ruyter, D. (2011). The relevance of cosmopolitanism for moral education. *Journal of Moral Education, 40*(11), 1–18.

Miller, D. (2002). Cosmopolitanism: A critique. *Critical Review of International Social and Political Philosophy, 5*(3), 80–85.

Moeller, S. D. (1999). *Compassion fatigue: How the media sell disease, famine, war and death.* New York: Routledge.

Murphy, L. (2000). *Moral demands in non-ideal theory.* New York: Oxford University Press.

Nash, R. J. (1997). *Answering the 'Virtuecrats': A moral conversation on character education.* New York, NY: Teachers College Press.

Neff, K. D. (2003). The development and validation of a scale to measure self-compassion. *Self and Identity, 2*, 223–250.

Neff, K. D. (2012). The science of self-compassion. In C. Germer & R. Siegel (Eds.), *Compassion and wisdom in psychotherapy* (pp. 79–92). New York: Guilford Press.

Neff, K. D., & Germer, C. K. (2013). A pilot study and randomized controlled trial of the mindful self-compassion program. *Journal of Clinical Psychology, 69*(1), 28–44.

Neff, K. D., & Pommier, E. (2012). The relationship between self-compassion and other-focused concern among college undergraduates, community adults, and practicing mediators. *Self and Identity.* doi:10.1080/15298868.2011.649546.

Neff, K. D., & Vonk, R. (2009). Self-compassion versus global self-esteem: Two different ways of relating to oneself. *Journal of Personaility, 77*(1), 23–50.

Neuberger, J. (2015, April 28). We must not turn a blind eye: These migrants deserve compassion. *The Guardian.* Online edition. http://www.theguardian.com/world/2015/apr/28/desperate-migrants-deserve-compassion. Accessed 14 Oct 2015.

Nietzsche, F. (1881/1997). *Daybreak: Thoughts on the prejudices of morality.* Edited by M. Clark & B. Leiter. Cambridge: Cambridge University Press.

Noakes, J. (2014). English. In J. Arthur, T. Harrison, & D. Wright (Eds.), *Teaching character through the curriculum: A guide to educating the virtues through and within 14 secondary school subjects* (pp. 18–21). Birmingham: Jubilee Centre for Character and Virtues.

Noddings, N. (1999). Caring and competence. In G. Griffin (Ed.), *The education of teachers* (pp. 205–220). Chicago: National Society for the Study of Education.

Noddings, N. (2001). Care and coercion in school reform. *Journal of Educational Change, 2,* 35–43.

Noddings, N. (2005). *The challenge to care in schools: An alternative approach to education.* 2nd edn. New York: Teachers College Press.

Noddings, N. (2012). The caring relation in teaching. *Oxford Review of Education, 38*(6), 771–781.

Norman, J., & Ganesh, J. (2006). *Compassionate conservatism: What it is, why we need it.* London: Policy Exchange.

Nouwen, H. (2009). *The way of the heart: The spirituality of the desert fathers and mothers.* San Francisco: Harper.

Nussbaum, M. C. (1996). Compassion: The basic social emotion. *Social Philosophy and Policy, 13*(1), 27–58.

Nussbaum, M. C. (2001). *Upheavals of Thought: The Intelligence of the Emotions.* Cambridge: CUP.

Nussbaum, M. C. (2004). Responses. *Philosophy and Phenomenological Research, 68,* 473–486.

Nussbaum, M. C. (2014). Compassion and terror. In M. Ure & M. Frost (Eds.), *The politics of compassion* (pp. 189–207). London: Routledge.

Olasky, M. (2000). *Compassionate conservatism: What it is, what it does and how it can transform America.* New York: The Free Press.

Osler, A., & Starkey, H. (2003). Learning for cosmopolitan citizenship: Theoretical debates and young people's experiences. *Educational Review, 55*(3), 243–254.

Owens, J. (1988). The self in Aristotle. *The Review of Metaphysics, 41*(4), 707–722.

Parekh, B. (2003). Cosmopolitanism and global citizenship. *Review of International Studies, 29*(1), 3–17.

Parker, W. C. (2003). *Teaching democracy: Unity and diversity in public life.* New York: Teacher's College Press.

Parker, W. C. (2006). Public discourses in schools: Purposes, problems and possibilities. *Educational Researcher, 35,* 8–18.

Payton, R., & Moody, M. (2008). *Understanding philanthropy: Its meaning and mission.* Bloomington: Indiana University Press.

Personal, Social and Health Education Association. (2015). *Teacher guidance: Preparing to teach about mental health and emotional wellbeing.* London: PSHEA.

Peters, D., & Calvo, R. A. (2014, September-October). Compassion vs. empathy: Designing for resilience. *Interactions, 21*(5), 49–53.

Peterson, A. (2009). Civic republicanism and contestatory deliberation: Framing pupil discourse within citizenship education. *British Journal of Educational Studies, 57*(1), 55–69.

Peterson, A. (2010). The formation and expression of character: Schools, families and citizenship. In J. Arthur (Ed.), *Citizens of character: New directions in character and values education.* Exeter: Academic Imprint.

Peterson, A. (2012). The educational limits of ethical cosmopolitanism: Toward a virtue theory of political and cultural cosmopolitan communities. *British Journal of Educational Studies, 60*(3), 227–242.

Peterson, A., & Bentley, B. (2016). Education for citizenship in South Australian public schools: A pilot study of senior leader and teacher perceptions. *The Curriculum Journal.* doi:10.1080/09585176.2016.1184579.

Peterson, C., & Park, N. (2009). Classifying and measuring strengths of character. In S. J. Lopez & C. R. Snyder (Eds.), *Oxford handbook of positive psychology* (pp. 25–34). New York: Oxford University Press.

Peterson, C., & Seligman, M. (2004). *Character strengths and virtues: A handbook and classification.* Washington: Oxford University Press.

Peterson, A., & Warwick, P. (2014). *Global learning and education: Key concepts and effective practice.* London: Routledge.

Piliavin, J. A. M., Dovidio, J. F., Gaertner, S. L., & Clark, R. D. (1981). *Emergency intervention.* New York: Academic Press.

Pogge, T. (2002). *World poverty and human rights.* Cambridge: Polity Press.

Pogge, T. (2005). Real world justice. *The Journal of Ethics, 9,* 29–53.

Popenoe, D. (1995). The roots of declining social virtue: Family, community and the need for a "Natural Communities Policy". In M. A. Glendon (Ed.), *Seedbeds of virtue: Sources of competence, character and citizenship in American society* (pp. 71–104). Lanham: Madison Books.

Putnam, R. D. (2015). *Our kids: The American dream in crisis.* New York: Simon & Schuster.

Richards, V. (2015). 5 practical ways you can help refugees trying to find safety in Europe. *The Independent.* http://www.independent.co.uk/news/world/eur ope/5-practical-ways-you-can-help-refugees-trying-to-find-safety-in-europe-10482902.html. Accessed 16 Feb 2016.

Rigoni, F. M. Fr (2007). Compassion and solidarity. *Social Work and Health Care, 44*(1–2), 17–27.

Rochester, C. (2006). *Making sense of volunteering: A literature review.* London: Volunteering England.

Rochester, C., Ellis Payne, A., & Howlett, S. (2009). *Volunteering and society in the 21st century*. Basingstoke: Palgrave Macmillan.

Rohrabacher, D. (2001, June 26). Paying homage to a special group of veterans, survivors of Bataan and Corregidor. *Congressional Record – House, V. 147, Pt. 9*, 11980–11985.

Ross, L. (1977). The intuitive psychologist and his shortcomings. In L. Berkowitz (Ed.), *Advances in experimental social psychology*. Vol. *10*. New York: Academic Press.

Rousseau, J.-J. (1755/1994). *Discourse on inequality* (trans: Philip, F, p. 17). Oxford: Oxford University Press.

Rousseau. J-J. (1755/2009). *Discourse on inequality*. Oxford: Oxford World Classics.

Rousseau, J.-J. (1762/1979). *Émile or on education* (Introduction, Translation and Notes by A. Bloom). USA: Basic Books.

Ruiz, P. O., & Vallejos, R. M. (1999). The role of compassion in moral education. *Journal of Moral Education, 28*(1), 5–17.

Ryan, T. (2010). Aquinas on compassion: Has he something to offer today? *Irish Theological Quarterly, 75*(2), 157–174.

Sanderse, W. (2013). The meaning of role modelling in moral and character education. *Journal of Moral Education, 42*(1), 28–42.

Sanderse, W. (2015). An Aristotelian model of moral development. *Journal of Philosophy of Education, 49*(3), 382–398.

Sanghera, B. (2016). Charitable giving and lay morality: Understanding sympathy, moral evaluations and social positions. *The Sociological Review, 64*, 294–311.

Schertz, M. (2007). Avoiding 'passive empathy' with philosophy for children. *Journal of Moral Education, 36*(2), 185–198.

Sherman, N. (1989). *The fabric of character. Aristotle's theory of virtue*. Oxford: Clarendon Press.

Singer, P. (1993). *Practical ethics*. 2nd edn. Cambridge: Cambridge University Press.

Smajdor, A. (2013). Reification and compassion in medicine: A tale of two systems. *Clinical Ethics*, 1–8. doi:10.1177/1477750913502620.

Smith, A. (2009[1759]). *The theory of moral sentiments*. R. P. Hanleyed. London: Penguin Classics.

Snow, N. (1991). Compassion. *American Philosophical Quarterly, 28*(3), 195–205.

Snow, N. (2000). Empathy. *American Philosophical Quarterly, 37*(1), 65–78.

Snyder, J. A. (2014, May 7). Teaching kids grit is all the rage. Here's what's wrong with it. *New Republic*. https://newrepublic.com/article/117615/problem-grit-kipp-and-character-based-education. Accessed 15 May 2016.

Solokon, M. K. (2006). *Political emotions: Aristotle and the symphony of reason and emotion*. Dekalb: Northern Illinois University Press.

Stebbins, R. (2004). Introduction. In R. Stebbins & M. Graham (Eds.), *Volunteering as leisure/leisure as volunteering: An international assessment.* Wallington: CABI Publishing.

Sverdlik, S. (2008). Compassion and sympathy as moral motivation. Occasional papers. Paper 3. http://digitalrepository.smu.edu/centers_maguireethics_occasional/3/. Accessed 25 Jan 2016.

Swedish National Agency for Education. (2000). *Democracy in Swedish education.* Stockholm: National Agency for Education.

Taggart, G. (2016). Compassionate pedagogy: The ethics of care in early childhood professionalism. *European Childhood Education Research Journal, 24*(2), 173–185.

Tagholm, R. (2015, August 24). 'Jungle' migrant camp in Calais now boasts library. *Publishing Perspectives.* http://publishingperspectives.com/2015/08/jungle-migrant-camp-in-calais-now-boasts-library/#.Vz7wwvkrLIU. Accessed 16 Feb 2016.

Taylor, C. (1992). The politics of recognition. In A. Gutmann (Ed.), *Multiculturalism and the politics of recognition* (pp. 25–74). Princeton: Princeton University Press.

Tobin, B. (1989). An Aristotelian theory of moral development. *Journal of Philosophy of Education, 23*(2), 195–211.

Unger, P. (1996). *Liberalism and affirmative obligation.* New York: Oxford University Press.

United Nations General Assembly. (2016). *One humanity: Shared responsibility. Report of the Secretary General for the World Humanitarian Summit.* http://sgreport.worldhumanitariansummit.org/. Accessed 20 Mar 2016.

United Nations Population Fund. (2016). *World humanitarian summit.* http://www.unfpa.org/events/world-humanitarian-summit. Accessed 30 May 2016.

Ure, M. (2014). Sympathy and antipathy in the extra-moral sense. In M. Ure & M. Frost (Eds.), *The politics of compassion* (pp. 230–247). London: Routledge.

Ure, M., & Frost, M. (2014). Introduction. In M. Ure & M. Frost (Eds.), *The politics of compassion* (pp. 1–17). London: Routledge.

Van Zomeren, M., Spears, R., Fletcher, A. H., & Leach, C. W. (2004). Put your money where your mouth is! Explaining collective action tendencies through group-based anger and group efficacy. *Journal of Personality and Social Psychology, 87*(5), 649–664.

Waldron, J. (2003). Teaching cosmopolitan right. In K. McDonough and W. Feinberg (Eds.), *Citizenship and education in liberal-democratic societies: Teaching for cosmopolitan values and collective identities* (pp. 23–55). Oxford: Oxford University Press.

Walker, D. (2015, April 25). I want leaders who look on migrants with compassion. *The Guardian.* Online edition. http://www.theguardian.com/commentisfree/2015/apr/25/bishop-of-manchester-leaders-look-on-asylum-seekers-with-compassion. Accessed 14 Oct 2015.

Weiner, B. (1980). A cognitive (attribution)-emotion-action model of motivated behaviour: An analysis of judgments of help-giving. *Journal of Personality and Social Psychology, 39*(2), 186–200.

Weaver, M. (2015, September 3, Thursday). Refugee crisis: What can you do to help? *The Guardian.* Online Edition. http://www.theguardian.com/world/2015/sep/03/refugee-crisis-what-can-you-do-to-help. Accessed 16 Feb 2016.

Welp, L. R., & Brown, C. M. (2014). Self-compassion, empathy, and helping intentions. *The Journal of Positive Psychology, 9*(1), 54–65.

Weng, H. Y., Fox, A. S., Shackman, A. J., Stockman, D. E., Caldwell, J. Z. K., Olson, M. C., et al. (2013). Compassion training alters altruism and neutral responses to suffering. *Psychological Science, 24*(7), 1171–1180.

White, R. (2008). Rousseau and the education of compassion. *Journal of Philosophy of Education, 42*(1), 35–48.

Whitebrook, M. (2014). Love and anger as political virtues. In M. Ure & M. Frost (Eds.), *The politics of compassion* (pp. 21–36). London: Routledge.

Wilde, S. (2013). *Care in education: Teaching with understanding and compassion.* New York, NY: Routledge.

Wilhelm, M. O., & Bekkers, R. (2010). Helping behaviour, dispositional empathic concern, and the principle of care. *Social Psychology Quarterly, 73*(1), 11–32.

Wilkinson, I. (2014). The new social politics of pity. In M. Ure & M. Frost (Eds.), *The politics of compassion* (pp. 121–136). London: Routledge.

Wuthnow, R. (1991). *Acts of compassion: Caring for others and helping ourselves.* Princeton, NJ: Princeton University Press.

Yoder, E. A. (2010). Compassion fatigue in nurses. *Applied Nursing Research, 23,* 191–197.

Yu, T. (2004). *In the name of morality: character education and political control.* New York: Lang.

Zagzebski, L. (2013). Moral exemplars in theory and practice. *Theory and Research in Education, 11*(2), 193–206.

INDEX

© The Author(s) 2017
A. Peterson, *Compassion and Education*,
DOI 10.1057/978-1-137-54838-2

Printed by Printforce, the Netherlands